363.2595 BOTZ
The nutshell studies of
unexplained death
Botz, Corinne May.
3334100444338

WITHDRAWN

P9-DWE-915

The Nutshell Studies *of Unexplained Death*

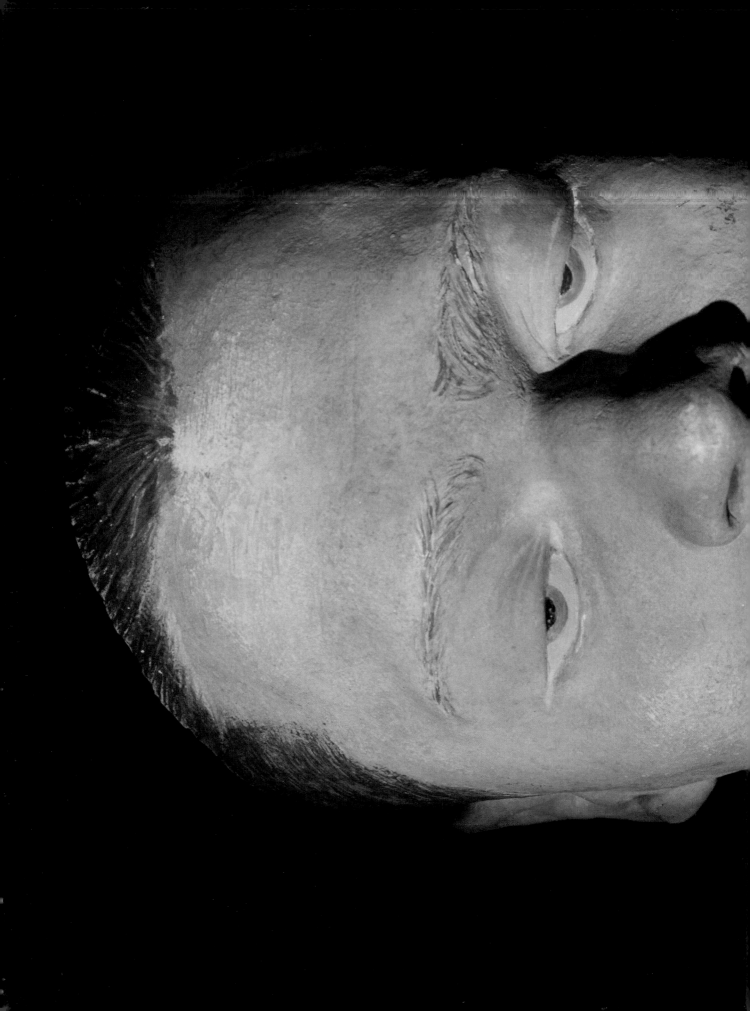

THE

Nutshell
Studies
of Unexplained Death

Essays and photography by
CORINNE MAY BOTZ

ALAMEDA FREE LIBRARY

CUTTHROAT HOMICIDE

To my parents, Jim and Leslie Botz,
who have always encouraged me to be and do
exactly what I want.

First published in the United States of America in 2004
by The Monacelli Press, Inc.
902 Broadway
New York, NY 10010

Copyright © 2004 The Monacelli Press, Inc.
Photographs © Corinne May Botz

All rights reserved under International and Pan-American Copyright
Conventions. No part of this book may be reproduced or utilized in any
form or by any means, electronic or mechanical, including photocopying,
recording, or by any information storage and retrieval system, without
permission in writing from the publisher. Inquiries should be sent to
The Monacelli Press.

The publishers have generously given permission to use extended quota-
tions from the following copyrighted works. From *The Invention of Solitude*,
by Paul Auster. © 1982 by Paul Auster. Reprinted by permission of Penguin
Books. From *The Collected Short Stories of Edith Wharton*, edited by R. W. B.
Lewis. © 1968 by William R. Tyler and Charles Scriber's Sons.

Library of Congress Cataloging-in-Publication Data
Botz, Corinne May.
The Nutshell Studies of Unexplained Death / Corinne May Botz.
p. cm.
ISBN 1-58093-145-6
1. Lee, Frances Glessner, 1878-1962. 2. Crime scene searches--Simulation
methods. 3. Homicide investigation--Simulation methods.
4. Crime scenes--Models. 5. Crime scenes--Models--Pictorial works.
6. Dollhouses--Pictorial works. I. Lee, Frances Glessner, 1878-1962. II.
Title.
HV8073.B648 2004
363.25'9523--dc22
2004007009

Printed by Graphicom Italia in Vicenza, Italy

Designed by Michael Worthington and Jon Sueda

The Nutshell Studies

CASE STUDIES

Appendix

INTRODUCTION

RICHARD B. WOODWARD

Writers of murder mysteries ask readers to identify with their main characters to an unusual degree. It is the mind of the detective that guides us around an often perilous fictional world supercharged with meanings. We have to decide whose perceptions of the case we can trust. Our senses should never stop tingling in case an offhand observation—the nicotine-stained fingers of the gamekeeper or a half-finished drink on a table—proves to be the thread that leads us out of the labyrinth of confusion and toward the solution. No noun, verb, or adjective can be overlooked in the text; and no character is entirely innocent—certainly not the detective—when everyone is a possible malefactor, victim, accomplice, witness, or font of clues, witting or not.

The genre is by tradition conservative. One of its lessons is that failing to interpret evidence correctly can be injurious or fatal. Whether private or on the public payroll, hard-boiled or genteel, investigators operate in what Baudelaire called "a forest of signs" and must be able to read a map of the relevant facts. No matter how left-wing their politics or messed up their private lives, detectives are restorers of order and comforters of the status quo. They often rely on predictive behavior—the laws of physics or the dog that failed to bark in the night—to catch a killer.

While demonstrating the intricate processes of reason, the writer of mysteries is often warning about its fragility or excesses. Being on constant alert for clues can overtax the mind. There is a fine line between the hypersensitivity of a C. Auguste Dupin or Sherlock Holmes and the dementia of paranoids, who find signs everywhere that others are plotting against them. Henry James understood the problem of misperception keenly and often flirted with the mystery form. In his stories "The Turn of the Screw," "The Beast in the Jungle," and "The Figure in the Carpet," he presented characters determined to find dramatic purpose or pattern in their own lives, whether it existed or not. Nabokov more openly satirized the conventions of the detective story by inventing madmen, like the confessed murderer Humbert Humbert in *Lolita* and the academic literary sleuth Charles Kinbote in *Pale Fire*, whose puzzle-solving acuity is a solipsistic trap that leads eventually to insanity and death.

Frances Glessner Lee was not crazy. But the eighteen dollhouses that she commissioned in the 1930s and '40s are touched with madness. At first it is hard to tell what we are looking at. Why is a female doll lying in a miniature bathtub underneath a faucet? Why is a man hanging by a noose in a barn? What is the meaning of the partially peeled potatoes? Of the worn line on the wall by the fallen chair? Who are these figures supposed to represent and what have they done? And, more puzzling, what mind created them?

Informed that these structures were called the "Nutshell Studies of Unexplained Death" and intended as training tools for detectives to help them better search for important evidence at crime scenes, we are still left with more clues than answers. The practicality of the dollhouses has over time become obscure. They are like a Victorian invention once heralded as progressive that now appears macabre and maybe a little unhealthy.

Even when Lee was alive, the idea that a mature woman had taken a fantasy plaything for little girls and turned it into a grim, bloodstained teaching tool for grown men must have seemed distinctly odd. Not that anyone would have dared to say so to her face. According to Corinne Botz's diligent research, Lee was a domineering figure who had a sense of humor as long as the subject was not herself. Still, she was sincerely dedicated to improving the techniques of criminal investigation and wealthy enough to deflect any questions about her motives. Shocking the innocent and plotting the crimes must have been fun for her. The dollhouses are in effect scenes from murder mysteries like those written by her friend Erle Stanley Gardner, except done in three dimensions and with meticulous attention to period detail. She was not just playing games either. As a well-born Chicago woman, she would have been expected to favor the style of Agatha Christie and Dorothy Sayers, in which the dead bodies, murderers, and detectives all tend to share a privileged background and the solution to the mystery relies more on logical ingenuity than knowledge of human nature. But Lee based her crime scenes on actual events that she learned about from police colleagues or read about in newspapers. The corpses in the dollhouses clearly suffered from too little money and hope. They may be only tiny dolls, but their clothes, furniture, and diet offer a more realistic picture of typical murder victims everywhere than the lives depicted in many classic detective stories.

How the study of a dollhouse contributed to actual police work is harder to say. The perspective of the investigator here is omniscient, which is never the case in solving crimes. During the week-long seminars at Harvard that Lee would host in the 1950s, with the "Nutshell Studies" as a centerpiece, detectives were given a slip of paper with a few relevant facts; from this paper and from observation they were then told to decide if the crime was a murder, suicide,

or accident. They couldn't reinterview witnesses, stake out a suspect, or do the gumshoe work that often results in the solution of crimes in the real world. What ill-paid policemen gained from invitations to these events, except the chance to play a parlor game and dine well at the Ritz, is not recorded. Probably Lee was as humored as much as she was respected.

Her most lasting legacy lies perhaps in the construction of these fantastic objects, which have now inspired an artist's astute interpretation. Just as Poe invented a detective before there were detective agencies, Lee seems to have anticipated a school of postmodern photography by creating environments where grim realism and childish whimsy collide. David Levinthal, Laurie Simmons, James Casebere, and Thomas Demand are a few who have explored the delirious artifice of scale models and toy worlds.

It is a tradition to which Corinne Botz now belongs. Her obsessiveness is a good match for Lee's. Photographing the Nutshell Studies and researching her subject was a seven-year project, one that Botz approached in the spirit of a detective on a cold but fascinating case.

Like readers of a well-told mystery story, we quickly learn to trust her photographic instincts. She would have been within her rights if she had shot the dollhouses in 1940s period black-and-white film noir style. Instead of clever parody, though, she chose warm, naturalistic color, a decision that heightens the weird intimacy and the dreaminess of these little death scenes. She takes note of the grotesque elements that tinge our present-day reading of Lee's enterprise, recognizing that the teaching aids have morphed into surrealist sculpture. But by viewing details in close-ups, Botz has also been respectful of the craft that went into the construction and that often reveals telling clues to the crime's solution.

I like to think that Lee, after some congenital grumpiness, would have appreciated Botz's modesty, intelligence, and devotion. She has examined the evidence with the thoroughness of a good police photographer and done a service to readers of detective fiction by reviving interest in a unique figure who deserves her own biography. Her pictures, like the dollhouses themselves, reward careful study. Deepening the sense of mystery about the woman who had them built at great expense, they are a reminder that all of our lives are potential crime scenes about which there will be many unanswerable questions.

Preface
ENCOUNTER

CORINNE MAY BOTZ

March 2004

While making a video about women who collect dollhouses, I met an obsessive collector who had hundreds of dollhouses but not a single doll. She explained that, as a prosecutor who deals with murder, rape, and child abuse on a daily basis, she didn't want to be reminded of humans and the awful crimes that they commit. "I create perfect worlds," she claimed. We had a lengthy conversation about her experience as a prosecutor and my interest in police photography. She insisted I visit a collection of crime-scene dollhouses at the Baltimore Medical Examiner's Office.

A week later I was standing in the little room on the third floor of the Medical Examiner's Office that houses the Nutshell Studies of Unexplained Death. I felt strangely at home and was drawn into this macabre universe, like a child lost in a book of fairy tales. I was entranced by the details: the porcelain doll with a broken arm in the attic, the grains of sugar on the kitchen floor, the fallen book with a flying witch on the cover. I was also riveted by the miniature corpses. Shot in bed, collapsed in the bathtub, hung in the attic, and stabbed in the closet; all were eternally frozen in miniature rooms that had become their tombs. I was disturbed by the prominence of female victims who had suffered violent deaths at home. Having recently moved from a cozy house in a small suburban town to a meagerly furnished apartment in a violent Baltimore neighborhood where rapes and sexual assaults occurred on a regular basis, I was perpetually afraid and spent much time thinking about the relationship between sex, violence, and space. I mentally crawled inside one of the rooms, slightly bigger than my hand, and thought for a moment (that felt like an hour), *I am dead.*

With the resolve of an investigator at the scene of a crime (yet with no interest in solving it), I began to photograph the models. Some say photographs "interrupt" the flow of time, yet taking pictures of the models made me feel like I was entering the moment, awaking the stasis, producing life. Perhaps this is the most fitting occasion to warn you that the photographs presented in this book are curiously unlike the models. Guilty myself of confusing my photographs of the models for the actual models, I am surprised each time I visit them. Like a person, the Nutshells appear to be continually changing—becoming more fragile, smaller, slightly larger, more obviously dead. My photographs simultaneously moved the models further from and closer to their source— the crime-scene photographs that guided their creation.

At the same time, my photographs moved me irrevocably toward the woman who made the Nutshells, Frances Glessner Lee. Her ghost has haunted me since the day I began to photograph the models, and, at moments, I felt sure she was creeping about inside them, daring me to find her one instant and demanding I leave the next. From the little I initially knew about her life, one thing was clear: we were unlikely collaborators. She was born into wealth ninety-nine years before I was born into the middle class. She constructed the Nutshells near the end of her life; I began to photograph them at the beginning of my working life. I identified with multiple perspectives when viewing them, but my primary interests were the victims and the loved ones I imagined they left behind; Lee embodied the characteristics of the classic detective: reason, detachment, and logic. What I referred to as "murder dollhouses," she considered scientific models.

I was influenced by Griselda Pollock's readings of the lives of canonical women artists. Pollock wrote, "Text by text, case by case, we read for the story of the other woman, to find through it not a 'great woman,' a heroine and idealized mother, but, in Freud's phrase, 'a [woman] like ourselves to whom we might feel distantly related.'"[1] Despite the disparities, I began to believe that, to understand myself artistically, I needed to try to see through the eyes of this woman to whom I felt "distantly related." Besides, she had begun to take up more space in my imagination than was reasonable for a stranger, and she wouldn't leave. Who was she? What kind of person would craft tiny models of murder scenes? Why, exactly, did she make them?

I set out to answer these questions, which seemed a simple enough task. But at some point, when I wasn't looking, the search took on a life of its own, and I was swept away with it. I walked through the houses where Lee lived and returned to photograph them. I scrutinized every detail in the models as if I were a palm reader and the details a line on Lee's hand. I stared for hours at a photograph of her as a young woman, willing the picture to come to life. I asked her grandchildren questions with a wavering voice and a far too timid demeanor. And on a cold May evening, I stooped over her grave, scrubbing at the mold on her headstone with the black cloth I use to take photographs. The next day I returned and made a rubbing to hang above my bed. I am her mirror as I rest beneath her gravestone.

Lee has become alive to me: I hear the sound of her voice and her gurgling, oppressed laugh. I watch her slip two thumbs in the front of her belt and move them side to side as she speculates with a stern and intimidating demeanor. I have a vision of her frolicking about her country estate as a child, a precocious little princess with a snake in her dress pocket.

But when it finally came time to assemble a narrative, I felt trepidation about telling her story and was filled with the wish that she would tell it for me. To complicate the matter, Lee and the Nutshells offered infinite stories and perspectives, entire volumes of stories inside stories, stories enough to eat you alive and stories enough to keep you alive. I finally decided to present a straightforward outline of her life, leaving some places untouched, making faint marks in others where a reader might decide to take over. I'm not sure I've answered the questions that spurred me on my quest. I simply tell this story rather than another, to regain possession of my life. In other words, the case is not closed.

1. Griselda Pollock, *Differencing the Canon: Feminist Desire and the Writing of Art's Histories* (New York: Routledge, 1999), 164.

Portrait of Frances Glessner Lee.

KILLING THE ANGEL
IN THE HOUSE:

The Case of Frances Glessner Lee

CORINNE MAY BOTZ

Frances Glessner Lee was a brilliant,

witty, shy, intimidating, and, by some accounts, impossible woman.
She gave what she thought you should have, rather than what you might actually want.

She had a wonderful sense of humor about everything and everyone, excluding herself. The police adored and regarded her as their "patron saint," her family was more reticent about applauding her, and her hired help was "scared to death of her." According to one family member, she could put you under the carpet in three words. Another remarked that she would "make a wonderful study for a psychiatrist." Lee embraced life's extremes and contradictions with utmost self-confidence (as just one example, she spent much of her life deliberately cultivating a scientific mentality, only to convert to Catholicism shortly before her death). Lee was a powerhouse who demanded that everything be executed according to her fully considered and precise plans. An article describes an incident in which a reporter repeatedly interrupted Lee during an interview. In response she "thrust her head slightly forward, pushed out her jaw and said, 'Look here, young man, you're trying to anticipate what I'm going to say, and you haven't the brains enough to do it.'"[1]

She was heavyset and didn't wear makeup; her hair was cut short, her ears were big, and her eyes penetrated the world from behind thin wire-frame glasses, noticing and remembering every detail. She favored a certain Queen Mary–style hat, black dress suits, and high collared blouses. Although she rarely wore jewelry, she never emerged without a watch on her wrist, in her pocket, and on her finger. She followed a regimented daily routine: breakfast at 8:30, lunch at 12:00, cocktails at 6:00, and dinner at 7:00. Lee seemed most at home when she was doing something that demanded exactitude—applying a small piece of yarn to a miniature spinning wheel or positioning a mouse fabricated from half a pussy willow bud into a trap. In these moments, her concentrated, serious demeanor seemed validated by her hands, which, though broad, sprouted fingers that her granddaughter Frances Heminway described as tapering to a fine point at the tips. She could accomplish any domestic task with these hands—sew, make lace, embroider, knit, or cook like a gourmet.

Despite her wealth, Lee belongs to the American tradition of self-taught, self-made individuals. Her poverty was the lack of opportunity to follow any but the path prescribed for young women of her social class. As a brilliant female forced to follow convention by her paternalistic family and society, she was almost another lost Shakespeare's sister; yet hers is the story of the late bloomer. In 1931, at the age of fifty-three, Lee underwrote a salary for a professor of legal medicine at Harvard, thus beginning a personal mission to improve crime detection in the United States. This marked a new era of Lee's life; as her daughter-in-law Percy Lee put it, she did not begin to live until her fifties. During the 1940s, Lee created the Nutshell Studies of Unexplained Death as part of her larger goal of improving the investigation of crime. More than fifty years later, the Nutshells are the most lasting evidence of Lee's achievements and continue to be used for teaching purposes. Their impact extends far beyond their intended purpose and offers a glimpse into the history of crime detection in the United States, domestic interiors of the 1940s, and cultural notions of gender and death. To understand and fully appreciate the Nutshells, it is necessary to consider their singular creator's life.

LIFE IN H. H. RICHARDSON'S GLESSNER HOUSE

Frances Glessner Lee was born on March 25, 1878, the second and last child of John J. and Frances Macbeth Glessner. Her parents had moved from Ohio to Chicago after their marriage, eventually settling on Prairie Avenue, Chicago's most elite address at the turn of the century, known as "the sunny street that holds the sifted few." Many of the prominent residents' names identified the source of their fortunes: Marshall Field's Department Store, the Pullman Palace Car Company, the Kimball piano manufacturers, and the Armour meatpackers. Lee's father was the cofounder and vice president of International Harvester, which then, as now, manufactures farm equipment. Glessner was active in countless clubs and associations and served as president of the Commercial Club and Citizen's Association and as trustee of the Chicago Orphan Asylum. Frances Glessner, who taught school before her marriage, efficiently managed the household while honing her skills as a pianist, seamstress, creator of silver jewelry and

objects, and beekeeper. She also hosted an exclusive reading group that congregated at her house every Monday for many years. As civic and cultural leaders of Chicago, Lee's parents exposed her to theater, art, and music and introduced her to prominent artists, intellectuals, and politicians. Frederick Law Olmsted, the landscape architect, and his wife were the Glessners' close friends, as were the president of Harvard and the conductor of the Chicago Symphony Orchestra.

The Glessners "were as devoted a couple as you would ever find anywhere in the world," Lee's daughter-in-law, Percy Lee, recalled. "They were more devoted to each other than they ever were to the children.... This made a great impact on Mrs. Lee especially."[2] An extremely bright, perceptive, and sensitive child, Lee was both indulged and reared, along with her brother, George, to exacting standards. She and George were both tutored at home. Although this gave Lee an exceptional education, she had few friends and rarely interacted with her contemporaries.

Lee's protected youth was reflected by the design of her childhood home. Designed by Henry Hobson Richardson and described by one critic as "pathologically private," Glessner House is a large granite structure, serious and austere, with few windows on the street facade and no front lawn.[3] The basement windows are barred, and, from the first, the house was equipped with an alarm system. A long corridor on the 18th Street side of the house allowed servants to access the front door without disturbing the family. The public rooms were oriented toward an enclosed courtyard with walls of windows that captured the southern light.[4]

The Glessners took great interest in each stage of the creation of their home. When it was erected in 1887, the house provoked an uproar in the neighborhood because it diverged drastically from the popular Victorian Revival–style architecture. People found the image of "home" conveyed by Glessner House aberrant and unsettling—some mistook it for an apartment building or a church; others compared it with a fort or a jail.[5] The most famous quote is George Pullman's: "I don't know what I have ever done to have that thing staring me in the face every time I go out my door."[6]

A dear old lady once said to me in all seriousness, "Mr. Glessner, you are a very important member of this community; you have a position of great prominence and influence; you get it from your wife and your house." Don't think this a disparagement of me. I thought it a real compliment, for I selected one, and I built the other.

JOHN GLESSNER, *The Story of a House*

TOP: The Glessner House courtyard, *Chicago*. BOTTOM: The Glessner House facade, *Chicago*.

Photograph Corinne Botz. Courtesy of Glessner House Museum, Chicago.

Mr. and Mrs. Glessner's bedroom, the Glessner House, *Chicago.*
Photograph Corinne Botz. Courtesy of Glessner House Museum, Chicago.

Dining room, the Glessner House, *Chicago.*
Photograph Corinne Botz. Courtesy of Glessner House Museum, Chicago.

This controversy simply strengthened the Glessners' devotion to the house. John Glessner's fondness for the structure led him to write *The Story of a House*, which he illustrated with photographs taken by his son. The book begins: "Mankind is ever seeking its comforts and to achieve its ideals. The Anglo-Saxon portion of mankind is a home-making, home-loving race. I think the desire is in us all to receive the family house from the past generation and to hand it on to the next with possibly some good mark of our own upon it. Rarely can this be accomplished in this land of rapid changes."[7]

This amply illustrates Glessner's bourgeois conception of the house as an expression of an ideal and of the advancement of civilization. In this view, both modernity and change threaten the home. By 1908 most elite residents were deserting Prairie Avenue and moving to the North Side, but nothing could persuade the Glessners to leave their beloved home, where they resided until their deaths in the 1930s. Mr. Glessner wrote *The Story of a House* in 1923, after the downfall of Prairie Avenue and the end of World War I.

The book provides a detailed account of the house and its contents. Mr. Glessner describes his home furnishings as having immense sentimental value—many had been handcrafted by friends, family, or famous artisans; some had been passed on from one generation to the next.[8] About their possessions Mr. Glessner says, "We don't realize how many they are and how much a part of us they are until we begin to catalogue them in our minds."[9] Their home philosophy and eclectic décor was influenced by the Arts and Crafts movement, which originated in Britain and advocated a return to a preindustrial sensibility in which artists handcrafted

one-of-a-kind, functional objects. Although the Glessners were industrialists, their interest in the Arts and Crafts movement articulated their fear of the leveling of the individual and culture through mass production. It also expressed their adherence to traditional, conservative values. As Joan Hansen wrote in her essay on the Glessners and the Arts and Crafts movement, "The home was not furnished as a showplace but as a refined, cultured and moral environment for the couple and their children."[10]

For her part, Frances Glessner kept a journal in which she recorded four decades of details of their household life. An excerpt from a typical entry, this one written near the time of Lee's marriage, reads:

Monday the reading class came—and in the afternoon F and I did errands. Tuesday dressmaking took the morning. In the afternoon I had over sixty calls. Wednesday dressmaking again. I went shopping with George in the afternoon. Frances [Lee] paid calls. Thursday dressmaking. In the evening we went to hear Nansen taking with us Mr. and Mrs. Birch and Mrs. Hurst. Frances and Mr. Lee went to the Dudleys to a dinner given to them. Friday dressmaking, and in the afternoon I went to the concert where Guilment played with the orchestra. The young people went to the Nelsons to a dinner given to them. Saturday at Weeks all morning. In the afternoon F. - went to the dentists, while I shopped. In the evening we went to the concert. Blewett and F - stayed at home. George went to Springfield. We had a blizzard.[11]

Kitchen, the Glessner House, *Chicago*. Located on the main floor, the kitchen was described by Mr. Glessner in *The Story of a House* as "well lighted, well ventilated, convenient, easily cleaned." Full-course dinners were sometimes prepared in the kitchen for over one hundred guests.
Photograph Corinne Botz. Courtesy of Glessner House Museum, Chicago.

Lee's mother thus meticulously recounted daily activities, including callers, shopping, meetings, theater, musicals, luncheons, dinners, art exhibits, and lectures. If she mentioned a social function, she carefully noted the names of the people who attended and the food served. She also preserved letters and invitations. The entries, however, are almost entirely devoid of personal impressions and emotions; they read like police reports.

The houses where Lee lived had an immense impact on her, and her experience of domestic space, in turn, informed the Nutshell Studies. Lee's childhood home is of particular importance, as it shaped her early consciousness, taste, and morals. The very creation of the models can be viewed as a continuation or perversion of her parents' obsession with their home. When Lee and her carpenter painstakingly handcrafted the contents of the models, she was echoing the Glessners' predilection for the handcrafted objects of the Arts and Craft

movement.[12] As Susan Stewart points out in *On Longing: Narratives of the Miniature, the Gigantic, the Souvenir, The Collection*, miniature objects are innately linked to "a pre-industrial labor, a nostalgia for craft" because they are usually handmade, unique objects.[13] Like the Glessner House interiors, the Nutshells represent rooms that are thoroughly designed, with harmoniously weaved furniture, ornament, textiles, colors, and patterns. Of course, unlike the Glessner House, the Nutshells represent interiors that someone of Lee's background would never call sophisticated.

To her mother, Lee owed her understanding of interior design, and from her mother and aunts she learned metalwork, sewing, knitting, crocheting, embroidery, and painting. Lee, however, relied on the limited knowledge and tools that society equipped her with as a woman to co-opt the feminine tradition of delighting in miniatures and dollhouses for decidedly unfeminine, scientific purposes. As Jennifer Doublet observed in her article on the Nutshells, "With something as seemingly innocuous and traditionally feminine as dollhouses [Lee] advanced in a male dominated field."

John Glessner's influence on his daughter was conflicted. Glessner operated successfully in the modern world through his lucrative business, yet he was able to dissociate himself from the working sphere in his home, where he relied on his wife to create a world apart. Throughout *The Story of a House*, Glessner emphasized that his wife was adept at making a home wherever they were staying: "She was a home-maker, a home-preserver—that was her first ambition, that was her most desired and profound success.... Wherever she went she took her workbag and work-basket and hung them in the room where she was, even in the sleeping cars, and they made the room a home."[14] The notion of a feminized home or the conflation of "woman" and "home" was popular throughout the Victorian era. Frances Glessner embodied this ideal, and John Glessner embraced it, effectively sentencing their daughter to a domestic life.

Stairwell in Main Hall, the Glessner House, *Chicago*. A portrait of H. H. Richardson hangs on the wall to the rear.
Photograph Corinne Botz. Courtesy of Glessner House Museum, Chicago.

By all accounts, however, despite their sharp division of labor and roles, the Glessners enjoyed a contented and egalitarian marriage. Lee, on the other hand, had to endure the negative ramifications of her parents' belief—which survived (or perhaps was strengthened by) her mother's stint as a teacher—that "a woman's place is in the home." Ironically, Lee's mother graduated from a teaching school and her father did not attend college. The first major blow came when her parents denied her a college education because her father believed "a lady didn't go to school."[15] Lucky brother George went off to Harvard.

Considering the rigorous curriculum Lee's tutors followed, her mother's activities in various educational clubs and societies, and the visibility of progressive female reformers (like Jane Adams) in Chicago in that era, it's little wonder that Lee wanted to attend college and "do something in my lifetime that should be of significant value to the community."[16] Medicine or nursing would have been her chosen field of study. Throughout her life, Lee resented the fact that she was not college-educated. She wrote at the age of seventy-three, "This has been a lonely and rather terrifying life I have lived. Chief amongst the difficulties I have had to meet have been the facts that I never went to school, that I had no letters after my name, and that I was placed in the category of 'rich woman who didn't have enough to do.'"[17]

In *A Room of One's Own*, Virginia Woolf theorizes about the influence of woman's limited experience on her art:

> *If Jane Austen suffered in any way from her circumstances, it was in the narrowness of life that was imposed upon her. It was impossible for a woman to go about alone. She never traveled; she never drove through London in an omnibus or had luncheon in a shop by herself. But perhaps it was the nature of Jane Austen not to want what she had not. Her gift and her circumstances matched each other completely. But I doubt whether that was true of Charlotte Bronte.*[18]

I also doubt whether that was true of Lee, for it was in her nature and training to feel entitled and to want more than she had. She was enraged and unremittingly bitter over the opportunities she was denied on account of her sex. According to her son, John, "Perhaps FGL should have been a man, at liberty to pursue a profession, required to earn a living, free from all the traditional shackles which restricted and infuriated her."[19] In Lee's case, unused intellect eventually inspired creativity, and oppression fueled near-obsession.

MIRROR HOUSES

On February 9, 1898, at the age of twenty, Lee married Blewett Lee in the parlor of the Glessners' house. Blewett, a lawyer and professor of law at Northwestern University, was from Mississippi. His father, Stephen D. Lee, had been a general in the Civil War, and, like his bride, Blewett had had a very sheltered upbringing.

After living at a number of Chicago residences, including 90 East 21st Street in what Lee described as "a nasty little apartment," Blewett and his wife moved into a town house at 1700 Prairie Avenue that the Glessners built for them. It sat beside an identical town house that the Glessners built for George and his wife. The houses were a gift, but they came at a price: the constant presence of Lee's nearby parents prevented her from creating an autonomous life with her husband. In addition to building them a house, the Glessners regularly gave them money to maintain the lifestyle Lee was accustomed to—a lifestyle that Blewett, at the start of his career, was unable to sustain. This created an additional obligation. According to their son, John, "The marriage, instead of being a liberating influence for FGL, resulted in even tighter ties to her family's control. Benevolent and kindly as such control was, it was none-the-less control."[20]

Lee gave birth to her first child, John, in 1902. She and Blewett separated soon after the birth of Frances, their second child, after four years of marriage. This separation, as John explained, was caused by an incompatibility in both interest and disposition: "Neither had much experience adapting to others. Also, she was probably spoiled by over-possessive parents. He was religious; she was not. His interests were almost completely indoors and intellectual, while hers also embraced the outdoors, and she had a creative urge coupled with high manual dexterity—the desire to make things—which he did not share."[21] Although the marriage would have probably failed regardless, John held the larger family situation responsible for making "the final breakup inevitable."[22]

Mirror houses built by the Glessners for their children on 1700 and 1704 *Prairie Avenue, Chicago.*
Courtesy of Glessner House Museum, Chicago.

Blewett moved into a nearby apartment above the residence of Lee's aunts. He and Frances managed to reunite long enough to conceive a third child, Martha. After the final separation in 1906, Lee wanted to get the divorce over and done with, but Blewett was not agreeable. The divorce finally took place in 1914. At the time of the divorce, Mr. Glessner sent Lee and her children to Santa Barbara with a staff of five people. This helped divert the attention of polite society from what was then considered a disgrace. The divorce permanently scarred Lee's relationship with her parents and her brother's family because she believed they sided with Blewett.

Although getting a divorce made Lee the authority figure in her home, this position was undermined by her financial dependence on her father, who was as controlling as ever with the money he allotted. When her son, John, was older, she told him of her financial needs and he relayed them to his grandfather. Lee's granddaughter, Frances Hemmway, recalled that, more than anything else, she wanted to get out from under her father's thumb. Perhaps she would have broken away from her family entirely if she had had the qualifications to support herself or if an inheritance were not looming in her future.

I've never been anywhere.
I've always sat at home, as though I were corked up in a bottle.
I'm to be married straight out of the bottle.

AGLAIA IVANOVNA in Fyodor Dostoyevsky's *The Idiot*

Despite appearances to the contrary, Lee had neither of the components that Virginia Woolf believed necessary for creativity: "a room of her own or five hundred a year."[23] The houses she resided in (in Chicago, Santa Barbara, Boston, and New Hampshire) were a constant reminder of her dependency and inability to support herself as an upper-class woman. Even worse, the money she received from her father demanded her restraint, burdened her with obligations, and reinforced her father's power over her life.

UNDER HER PARENTS

Lee had spent each summer of her childhood at the Rocks, the family's thousand-acre estate in Littleton (now Bethlehem), New Hampshire.[24] (She would move there permanently when her children were grown.) The country house epitomized the preindustrial lifestyle espoused by the Arts and Crafts movement. The Glessners meticulously transformed the barren, rocky landscape into a working farm with nearly two dozen specialized buildings, each carefully designed, sited, constructed, and named.[25] A working farm, the Rocks was also in keeping with the Arts and Crafts appeal for self-sufficiency. Frederick Law Olmsted designed the terrace gardens. As a child, Lee took an active part in the construction of the buildings and wrote, "I have nailed shingles on every roof on the place."[26]

As an adult, Lee, together with her children, three maids, and a nurse, lived in the Cottage, a dwelling originally built to house the gardener. Living at the Cottage allowed Lee to place the greatest possible distance between herself and her parents and her brother's family. When even the Cottage did not provide Lee with ample privacy, she purchased the Camp, a small house an hour away where she often escaped with her children to "get out from under her parents."[27] Perhaps to reinforce the idea of the Camp as an escape, Lee and her children called each other by different names when they were there. Lee's son remembered, "These were the happiest times of my childhood. FGL was always gay and cheerful and companionable. Once she undertook to sing opera, all the parts, with gestures. Then there were stories—long adventure stories we made up and told each other, usually at mealtime. Suddenly the storyteller would stop and it was up to the next in turn to continue then and there."[28] According to Lee's son, "When not oppressed by the family situation, FGL was very good company for her children, unless she was involved in a

project. These were all-absorbing, and FGL would work all day and half the night for weeks at a time."[29]

In 1913 Lee made her first model, a miniature version of the Chicago Symphony Orchestra, as a birthday gift for her mother who, along with John Glessner, was a lifelong supporter of the Chicago Symphony. Lee created dolls representing each of the ninety musicians and outfitted them with the appropriate miniature instruments—some of which had accompanying cases. To prepare for her work, she attended rehearsals to observe the musicians, which enabled her to personalize some of the dolls, especially those meant to represent close friends of the Glessners. The musicians displayed the score for the concert on their music stands. Lee even created and bound a miniature program book. The lapel of each tuxedo jacket held a flower, just like the one Frances Glessner customarily sent to the musicians to wear during performances. As their real-life counterparts did in Orchestra Hall, the dolls sat on tiers within a wooden stage, which, in this case, were approximately eight feet wide and four feet deep. Lee completed the work in two months.

It took her two years to complete her next and more elaborate model of the Flonzaley Quartet. These dolls bore an uncanny resemblance to their breathing counterparts. Incredibly, some of the miniature instruments even produced a sound (all looked as if they could). Lee's son, then twelve years old, assisted her. He later remembered, "We went to concerts together and sat at opposite sides of the house and made elaborate notes on how the men sat and what they wore—Mr. Betti's vest (he was the first violin), how Mr. Pochon put his feet (he was the second violin), d'Archambeau's gold watch-chain, how it hung (he, the cellist) and last, but by no means least, Ugo Ara, who played the viola, a little Italian man with a magnificent Assyrian beard, how he managed his viola amongst the profusion of shrubbery."[30] The conductor of the Chicago Symphony composed the score that sat on the music stands, but, in jest, he made certain it would be impossible to play.

On the night of the grand unveiling, the quartet joined the Glessners for dinner. The model was hidden on the table beneath a floral piece. After they finished dinner, Lee and her father unveiled the model. John vividly recollects: "For a moment nobody spoke, and then all four members of the quartet broke out into voluble language. Nobody listened. But each one of them pointed with delight to the eccentricities of the other three."[31]

Another important activity that prefigured the Nutshells occurred in 1919, when Lee volunteered to arrange

Bridge Barn, the Rocks estate, *Bethlehem, N.H.*

transportation home for soldiers returning from World War I and their temporary living quarters on Beacon Hill in Boston. Her task surrounded her with uniformed men, an experience she would later repeat by surrounding herself with uniformed policemen. Moreover, analogous to the detective who solves crimes and restores domestic harmony, Lee had the satisfaction of working behind the scenes to reunite soldiers with their families.

Lastly, during the 1920s, Lee and her daughter Frances ran an antique shop at the Rocks. Following the path of antique pickers everywhere, they drove around the countryside knocking on the doors of farmhouses to buy furniture that they would later fix up and resell. By indulging Lee's longstanding interest in home decoration and introducing her to a wide variety of New England homes and furniture, this venture gave Lee valuable knowledge to draw on for her Nutshell Studies.

DEATH AND FULFILLMENT

Lee's brother died in 1929, her mother in 1932, her daughter in 1935, her father in 1936, and her close friend Dr. Magrath in 1938. After Lee's father died she finally came into her inheritance and could control every aspect of her life. She inherited half of the Rocks estate (the other half was given to her late brother's family) and assumed responsibility for operating the farm. She demolished her parents' house, known as the Big House, in 1946 and her brother's house, the Ledge, in 1947. From that point forward, Lee's humble cottage was the focal point of the Rocks. Although Lee had become active in legal medicine in the early 1930s, her father disapproved, so it was not until after he died that her career began to flourish.

Lee became involved in legal medicine late in life, but she had met the man who would become the driving force behind her passion when her brother, George, came home from Harvard for a vacation with a medical student friend, George Burgess Magrath, in tow. Magrath was a charismatic, eccentric, dashing redhead, and Lee was enamored. It's easy to imagine her, as a young woman, sitting in the parlor near the fireplace, eyes aglow, mouth slightly agape, listening as Magrath circled the room with his signature large curvy pipe, telling tales of real-life murder. Lee and Magrath developed a friendship that continued in the years to follow. Magrath went on to serve as medical examiner of Suffolk County (Boston), solving notorious murder cases throughout New England and becoming a sought-after expert witness in courtrooms throughout the United States.[32] Lee paid close attention to his career. What's more, she never forgot his stories.

According to Lee's daughter-in-law, Percy Lee, her interest in crime was due to her interest in Magrath. As Lee herself recalled in a letter, in the 1930s, she and Magrath had had a conversation about the need to improve training for those investigating sudden and violent deaths. The schools (such as the one at the FBI) that taught police science had overlooked the medical approach to homicide training. Indeed, despite the vital importance of the medical aspect of a homicide investigation, only a few states required coroners, who assign a cause and manner of death, to obtain a medical degree. Instead, the local coroner was usually an undertaker or had been elected for political reasons. This meant that innumerable murders went undetected because of mishandled evidence and a failure to perform autopsies, since, lacking medical knowledge, the coroners easily missed subtle indications of violent death. Jürgen Thorwald, author of *The Century of the Detective*, described the coroner system in the United States during this time as "hopelessly defective."[33]

Today medical examiners are physicians who investigate sudden, unexpected, or violent deaths. Autopsies

While I know it is said that there is no one in the world whose place cannot be filled, still I believe that Legal Medicine will take something of a slump when I die, for, though I say it myself, I have had enthusiasm, willingness, courage, patience, and persistence, and believe my personality has been effective in what I have been trying to accomplish.

FRANCES GLESSNER LEE, *letter to the Advisory Board of the Frances Glessner Lee Trust*

are performed to identify the deceased and determine the cause (disease, injury, or substance), the manner (natural, suicide, homicide, or accident), and the method of death. The autopsy report supplies crucial leads for crime-scene investigators, and, if the case is tried, the physician usually presents the autopsy findings and his or her conclusions in court.

Replacing the office of coroner with a medical examiner or amending the laws under which the coroner worked became one of Lee's central aims. She believed that every state should and would one day have the medical examiner's system.

Lee saw this as her first opportunity to "do something in my lifetime that should be of significant value to the community."[34] As she explained in a letter:

> First, I am, and always have been, a lone worker and have never found it satisfactory to work at something that has been gone over and over by others until the original meaning and spirit have all been worn out of it. Therefore when an opportunity came to me to start something completely new in the medical line, I was delighted to take it on. As a girl, I was deeply interested in medicine and nursing and would have enjoyed taking a training in either one. This was not possible, so Legal Medicine, including medicine and just ordinary common sense, together with some smattering of detective work, made an immediate appeal to me. However, I found that no one, including alas! my own self, knew exactly what Legal Medicine was supposed to mean, and at the time—around 1930—that I first became active in its development, there was very little printed material available to help me. So it was necessary to proceed by main strength and awkwardness, but fortunately with the skill, knowledge and training of Dr. Magrath to guide me (he, in turn, really started from scratch), I have been able to accomplish a good deal.[35]

In 1931–32, Lee, who had been denied a Harvard education by her family, underwrote a salary for a professor of legal medicine at Harvard. Dr. Magrath was the first to hold the Chair.[36] Two years later, she established the George Burgess Magrath Library of Legal Medicine at Harvard, which included over one thousand rare and one-of-a-kind books that she had collected. At the dedication ceremony she declared, "My wish is to build up here a Department of Legal Medicine second to none, but its growth must be gradual in order to be sure. The plan is destined to a manifold development, only a small part of which is as yet under way. We are here today… to lay the cornerstone of a structure which will need time to build, but which must ultimately prove of consequence in the service of mankind."[37]

In 1936 Lee established the George Burgess Magrath Endowment of Legal Medicine with an endowment of $250,000.[38] Although Lee never received formal training, she became a respected authority in the field, and, as a consultant to the department, her views helped mold its agenda. During Lee's lifetime, the department concentrated on the medical-legal perspective of homicide investigation by providing residency training for doctors to become medical examiners (with additional funding from the Rockefeller Foundation), arranging conferences and seminars on medico-legal techniques, conducting autopsies, publishing research findings, and offering a course in forensic medicine to medical students at Harvard, Tufts, and Boston University. In part as a result of the conferences and of pioneering legislation proposed and promoted by Lee, seven states amended their coroner system.[39]

Though students in the department would have benefited greatly from hands-on training, this was impossible because of time restraints, the unlikelihood of a crime occurring during training sessions, and laws that prohibited disclosing details of an unsolved crime to members of the public. More than anything else, these impediments led Lee to create the teaching tool she called the Nutshell Studies of Unexplained Death, after a well-known police saying: "Convict the guilty, clear the innocent, and find the truth in a nutshell." The Nutshells were miniature crime scenes created from composites of actual cases that Lee, police colleagues, and Dr. Magrath investigated. According to Alton Mosher (Lee's carpenter), who often accompanied her, if the case didn't interest her as a potential model, she didn't want any part of it. She selected the most enigmatic cases to baffle the detectives-in-training and teach them that nothing should be taken at face value: murders can be staged as accidents or suicides, suicides can masquerade as accidents, and accidents can be misconstrued as murder. The models present cases that are impossible to solve with visual evidence alone. Instead, the fact that vital clues must be derived from autopsies and from the results of lab tests highlights the importance of the need for communication among the medical examiner, law enforcement officers, and forensic investigators at the scene of the crime.

Tenth seminar in homicide investigation, *Harvard Medical School.*
Lee is seated at the head of the table; her daughter, Martha Batchelder, is two seats from her right. Standing directly behind Batchelder
is Erle Stanley Gardner, who attended the seminar and spoke at the Ritz Carlton dinner. Gardner praised the seminar in the foreword to his book
The Case of the Dubious Bridegroom, which he dedicated to Lee.

MOTHER AND SONS

In 1945 Harvard inaugurated the Frances Glessner Lee Seminars on Legal Medicine and installed the first models.[40] Lee organized every aspect of the seminars, which were held by the Department of Legal Medicine to train police officers. She took a special interest in training police officers because, as the first to arrive on the scene of a crime, they had to recognize and preserve evidence critical to solving the case. At the time, most police officers inadvertently botched cases by touching, moving, or failing to identify evidence. Lee was also extremely interested in better integrating the work of and communication among medical experts, police officers, forensic investigators, and prosecutors. "My whole object," Lee explained, "has been to improve the administration of justice, to standardize the methods, to sharpen the existing tools as well as to supply new tools, and to make it easier for the law enforcement officers to 'do a good job' and to give the public 'a square deal.'"[41]

Held twice a year, the seminars lasted an entire week. Lee brought in experts from around the world to speak and invited twenty-five to thirty police officers to attend. Lee's friend Erle Stanley Gardner, creator of the *Perry Mason* series, observed, "Invitations to attend are as sought after in police circles as bids to Hollywood by girls aspiring to be actresses."[42] Lee carefully considered every detail, from the order of topics discussed to conditions in the departmental library where the classes were held, which provided "a feeling of home-likeness and informality so essential to the success of the course."[43]

The seminars covered all aspects of a homicide investigation, including methods of determining the time of death, the difficulties of identifying victims, the interrogation of suspects and witnesses, and an autopsy. Participants also had the benefit of a training session in which they analyzed two of the Nutshell Studies for an hour and a half each under Lee's watchful gaze. Her presence allowed her to answer questions while enjoying the sight of burly policemen hovering in stupefaction over her delicate creations.

The officers took notes on the Nutshell cases as they would at a homicide investigation and later made a verbal report to the class, drawing attention to objects that might yield important clues (cigarettes, food, weapons), details that seemed out of place, and evidence of medical importance. Although they commonly presented a few hypotheses regarding how the victim died (natural death, suicide, homicide, or accident) and defended their ideas with details from their observations, they were not supposed to treat the Nutshells as "whodunits." As Lee noted, "The Nutshells Studies are not presented as crimes to be solved—they are, rather, designed as exercises in observing and evaluating indirect evidence, especially that which may have medical importance."[44]

The policemen raved about the seminars. William P. Hancock, attendee of the tenth seminar and retired captain of the Maine State Police, went to many training schools, including the FBI academy, but he rated the Harvard seminar superior for its purposes of homicide investigation. The attendees attested that they utilized what they learned on future cases, and some held it responsible for their promotions. The policemen made contacts at the seminar, which were invaluable if a case they investigated led them to a different state. Due to the success of the seminars, Lee began to organize training courses for police schools in various states.

I think I can promise you that I will stay right here with Legal Medicine, and with the State Police, until I drop dead in my tracks!

FRANCES GLESSNER LEE, *age seventy-one, 1949 meeting of the Harvard Associates in Police Science*

When Lee became involved with police work, law enforcement agencies were inaccessible to ordinary civilians in general and to women in particular. "Men are dubious of an elderly woman with a cause," explained Lee. "My problem is to convince them that I am not trying to butt in or to run anything. Also, I have to sell them on the fact that I know something of what I am talking about."[45] Despite her initial struggles, however, Lee eventually became known as "the patron saint of policemen and policewomen." In 1942 she was appointed a captain in the New Hampshire State Police with the title of Education Director, which allowed her to become the first woman to join the International Association of Police Chiefs.[46]

Lee's career satisfied her desire to preside over a small entourage of handsome, polite young men dressed in uniforms. No one could talk her out of anything except, according to her granddaughter, Frances Heminway, "a very handsome young man who had impeccable manners."[47] Photographs exist of Lee sitting regally at the head of the table at dinners and police seminars, the only woman surrounded by thirty or so policemen, or enveloped by a small group of attentive officers. In these photographs, her habitually severe demeanor is softened, her eyes twinkle, and her smile is radiant. Given the available choice of male-female relationships that could explain this phenomenon, Lee chose the one that most comfortably fit her age and social status: "The relationship which has developed between the State Police Students and me is a truly unique one—they all call me Mother and to me they are all Son."[48] Each year on Mother's Day, Lee received a stack of cards from the policemen.[49] "She became absolutely enamored [with the policemen] because they made so much of her," Percy Lee recalled. "They thought she was a mother figure, and this pleased her to no end…. She always had a young man around whom she treated that way [like royalty], to my husband's great disgust." Lee converted to Catholicism near the end of her life because of the policemen's influence.

Frances Glessner Lee didn't like women. Some of her family members say she simply related better to men, but her great-granddaughter Virginia Lee surmised that her ties with the policemen might have been a way of attaining "all that male recognition that her father hadn't given her."[50] Lee played the role of mother hen with the policemen, a guise she never assumed with her children or grandchildren.

She often rode around with the policemen on their cases, had a pipeline into cases being investigated in various states, and corresponded with countless officers. When she visited policemen in a distant state, she was escorted from state to state, or county to county, by the officers. The policemen invariably describe Lee as gracious, a mother to law enforcement agents, a mentor and a good, kind friend. Many were in awe of her position and intelligence. "Mrs. Lee was truly one of the most exceptional persons I have ever met," stated William F. Baker, a graduate of the seminar. "To have been her friend for 12 years will forever stand out in my mind as one of the most rewarding experiences of my life. Law enforcement [has] never had a better or more sincere ally."[51] For her part, Lee wrote, "They have been wonderfully dear and sweet to me and have brought a beautiful happiness to my last years."[52] Her funeral was lined with policemen and there were two separate services: a church service for the policemen and her Catholic associates, and a nondenominational memorial service at the house for her family.

In keeping with her maternal role, Lee hosted a banquet for the attendees of the police seminars. Held at the Ritz Carlton, the dinner was carried out with "conspicuous elegance, generosity and friendship," according to Lee.[53] The meal was served on an $8,000 set of dishes that Lee had the Ritz purchase and use only for this event. The Ritz manager, Charles L. Banino, remembered, "She treated her guests as if they were royalty. They could have anything they wanted and as much as they wanted—as long as they behaved like gentlemen." Her instruction to the wine steward was: "Shut off anyone who talks in a loud voice."[54] For the policemen, many of whom came from small towns and modest backgrounds, it was a grand and unforgettable affair. "It was beyond anything that I ever had the pleasure of attending," Baker stated. He recounted how Lee individually greeted each officer at the dinner: "She wanted to know our background, whether we were married or not, what we thought of police work, why we got involved in police work, whether we enjoyed police work or not."[55] Her son, John, remarked about a dinner he attended: "FGL herself was on the top of the wave. Busy, interested and interesting, and able to make some witty remarks at dinner. There were always two or three clustered around her chair afterwards when there were drinks. She gave the impression of being a good ten years younger than usual. I suspect, though, that she was a pretty tired lady when it was all over; she was 76 at the time."[56] The dinners were part of Lee's effort to foster social networking among the seminar attendees. She took great care in assigning the seating so that each officer would find himself placed beside an officer from a different state with whom Lee thought he could form a friendship and thereby strengthen the national police network.

In 1946 graduates of the first seminar held a meeting at the Department of Legal Medicine and formed an organization called Harvard Associates in Police Science (H.A.P.S.). The object of the group, which holds annual meetings, is to bring together individuals who have completed the seminar for a refresher course, to reinforce the information they learned at the seminar and introduce the latest techniques and procedures in crime prevention and detection.

Today, anyone can be an amateur sleuth. For those who watch popular forensic television programs, the meaning of luminol and the significance of trace evidence is common knowledge. In fact, forensics is quickly becoming part of high school curriculums across the country. In the past few years, the desire to "convict the guilty and clear the innocent" has dramatically increased. While the Nutshells offer a glimpse into crimes and detection of a past era, they continue to be a valuable teaching tool because the ability to properly identify, evaluate, and preserve evidence at the crime scene remains a critical part of an investigation. The O. J. Simpson case, with its slipshod handling of evidence, is a case in point. *Henry Lee's Crime Scene Handbook* states, "It seems ironic that while forensic science has experienced significant advances and improvements, the utilization of forensic science is still at the mercy of the crime scene investigator. If the crime scene is not properly managed, all of the technology and advances we currently possess and will possess in the future will be unable to overcome these shortcomings, and justice will continue to be unattainable in far too many cases."[57] Lee was ahead of her times in identifying this problem and establishing training courses for law enforcement officers.

In 1967, four years after Lee's death, the Harvard Department of Legal Medicine closed for financial reasons. With the support of Lee's family, Russell Fisher, M.D., previously a professor of legal medicine at Harvard and then chief medical examiner in Maryland, arranged for the transfer of the Nutshells to the Medical Examiner's Office in Baltimore, where they are on permanent loan. In 1992 the Maryland Medical-Legal Foundation, caretaker of the models, provided $50,000 to have them restored. The police seminars continue to be held twice a year at the Maryland Medical Examiner's Office. They attempt to replicate Lee's seminar by bringing in various speakers, having a training session with the Nutshells and a banquet (albeit not at the Ritz). According to David Fowler, M.D., Maryland's chief medical examiner, "The Nutshells have always epitomized the commitment of many, including Frances Glessner Lee, to educating death investigators to a disciplined and accurate investigation, which is critical in supporting the bereaved, as well as the criminal justice and public heath systems. There is still in today's world no equal in 'virtual reality' that can compare with the models." Every graduate of the seminar becomes a member of the Harvard Associates in Police Science, which continues to hold annual conferences.

Frances Glessner Lee standing with policemen.

CONSTRUCTION
OF THE
NUTSHELL STUDIES

Frances Glessner Lee working on the Nutshell Studies.

Lee created the Nutshell Studies of Unexplained Death at the Rocks, in an enormous four-story farmhouse complete with elevator. The elevator doors opened on the second floor to reveal a carpenter's workshop. Beyond this was a large room filled with dressers containing miniatures that Lee had collected during her travels around the world: bedroom furniture, kitchen accessories, mirrors, light fixtures, shrubs, cars, fabrics, et cetera. Sometimes Lee acquired multiples of the same type of miniature to cover every possible difference in what ordinary people might consider minute, insignificant details; for example, she might have twenty imported toy cars with only slightly different styles and colors. Only a small portion of the enormous collection would eventually find its way into the Nutshell Studies, yet Lee carefully guarded the room, sternly instructing visitors not to touch a thing.

Lee's workshop was just beyond the miniature room. This was where she hunched to knit stockings with needles the size of ordinary straight pins, a task so arduous she could only complete a few rows at a time. This was where she would prepare her dolls, carefully sticking a knife into a lower abdomen, painting a face the crimson pink of carbon monoxide poisoning, or suspending a "corpse" from a noose.

Lee combined the full gamut of her expertise and talent to create the models: the interest in interior design she garnered from her mother, home decorating books, and the antique shop she operated with her daughter; her painstaking attention to detail; her gift for handiwork; and her knowledge of crime detection and legal medicine. With the assistance of her carpenter, Ralph Mosher, who assisted Lee from 1943 until his death in 1951, when he was succeeded by his equally talented son, Alton,[58] she constructed approximately three Nutshell Studies per year. Each individual model incorporated elements, or "problems," from various crime scenes: each is a composite. Everything depicted happened, but nothing occurred exactly as shown. Working from photographs, measurements, and police reports, she often changed the location of the crimes as well as names and dates, and "enlarged [the facts] to create a more intricate problem."[59] While the interiors do not replicate actual crime scenes, sometimes Lee chose to match particular design elements to the scene of the crime (for instance, she might give her carpenter a crime-scene photograph with a piece of furniture in it that she wanted built).

As soon as Lee conceived of a master plan for one of the models, her carpenter drew a blueprint according to her specifications, reducing the measurements to the scale of one inch to one foot. *Barn, Log Cabin, Burned Cabin, Garage, Three-Room Dwelling*, and *Two-Story Porch* are freestanding models that include interior and exterior views. The remaining twelve models are three-sided containers with a roof (the fourth side is open for viewing).

Her carpenter needed, as Lee put it, "infinite patience and precision and also a tinkerer's aptitude."[60] He equated the length of time he spent building a single model as equivalent to that required to build a house. For Lee, time

Capt. Lee was a perfectionist in every sense of the word.... I don't think there was any detail too small or too insignificant to be given careful, painstaking consideration.

ERLE STANLEY GARDNER, *Boston Globe*, 1962

and money were irrelevant. The only thing that mattered was that every single detail was realistically and precisely executed. She believed that if the policemen noticed imperfections, they would question the credibility of the crime and, by extension, her credibility. The attention to detail was also essential because the viewer had to believe on some level that the dioramas were real. Lee knew they must "experience what is large in what is small"[61] in order to take them seriously. Lee's desire for perfection led her to consult with numerous model makers for help building specific items and to correspond with physicians at the Harvard Medical School to ensure that everything anatomical was scientifically correct. The models are facsimiles of life, and everything works—window shades, a mousetrap, whistles, pencils, a tiny stereoscope (Lee incorporated a set of photographs, reduced from originals and placed on a sliding rack). When she used a miniature coffeepot, she equipped it with a strainer complete with coffee grinds.[62]

When beginning a model, Lee scoured her miniature collection for appropriate items. Sometimes she was content with store-bought dollhouse furniture. The German Biedermeier company, for example, made the pier table in the foyer of *Parsonage Parlor*, which boasts an imitation rosewood finish, gilt trim, and marble top; Lynnfield crafted the cabinet, table, and breakfast nook in *Kitchen*; and Tynietoy provided the green spool bed and dresser in *Striped Bedroom*. Lee also refashioned commonplace objects to serve her purpose: a Cracker Jack prize became a little girl's toy rocking horse, a Benzedrine inhaler made a perfect fire hydrant, and the charm from a necklace metamorphosed into an eggbeater.

In most cases, Lee disassembled and altered the dollhouse furniture she used because her models required "the utmost accuracy and fidelity in dimension and proportion."[63] She stripped and repainted tiny tables and chairs and reupholstered couches in material of a fine-scale weave in a pattern in keeping with the style of the room. Her carpenter made much of the furniture from scratch, using jeweler's tools, dental instruments, and a large magnifying glass to accomplish his small-scale feats. He would use a jigsaw to transform picture-frame moldings into cornices, doors, and windows. Each door has working hinges and a working key.

Lee carefully choose the color and design of the wallpaper to reflect the victim's lifestyle and create the appropriate atmosphere in the rooms. She spent countless hours searching through sample books at wallpaper stores to find the "right" wallpaper. Then she would purchase a huge roll, from which she would select a small portion of the pattern for her carpenter to cut into twelve-inch strips (so the wallpaper strips would be proportioned) and hang in the miniature rooms. Her choices ranged from a quaint pattern of farmers and animals to a dreamy underwater scene to a dramatic red with roses. Lee used bare cement walls to create *Unpapered Bedroom*, a drab, second-rate hotel room housing an unidentified victim.

Irving & Casson—A. H. Davenport Company, the Boston interior-decorating firm, was a key supplier of Lee's material,[64] and she sometimes commissioned the company to fashion miniature items (two watch crystals, silvered pieces of glass, and a small drawing in the likeness of a *New Yorker* cover, et cetera).[65] Lee requested catalogs from manufacturers when she didn't have photographs or measurements of an item she wanted. If the catalogs didn't offer adequate detail, she might go so far as to place a "Wanted" ad in the local newspaper, requesting permission to photograph and measure a specified piece of furniture. She ordered bisque doll parts from the New York Doll Hospital, "very thin and light weight" fabrics with small patterns from textile manufacturers, pictures like those used in picture puzzles from lithographers, and Crab Orchard and Town Tavern whiskey labels from the National Distillers Corporation.

The dollhouse company Cranford Miniatures was an invaluable source of supplies. One order included corn on the cob, a dictionary, bathroom scales, kitchen tools, a dishpan set, and a Mixmaster. Despite her seeming unconcern with expense and her capacity to store items, she placed another order with the understanding that she might return some items, as, due to the "meager" and "vague" description of their sizes, she was uncertain if they would suit her models. Lee instructed the company, "The standard measurements in a furniture store of a chair is the height of the seat from the floor, and the fiddle back side chair you have listed is described as 3-3/4" high. On a scale of one inch to one foot, that would make the chair 3'9" from the floor. If this dimension is the height of the back of the chair, it is higher than any Fiddle back chair in my possession."[66] Lee softened, or perhaps reinforced, her criticism by sending the company a gift along with the letter: a custom-made scale ruler (like the one she used in her work), which easily translated measurements in feet and inches to the one-inch-to-one-foot scale.

THE DOLLS: DEFINITELY DEAD

Lee made each miniature corpse and its clothing herself. She began with loose bisque heads, upper torsos, hands meant for German dolls, and with carved wooden feet and legs. She attached these loose body parts to a cloth body stuffed with cotton and BB gun pellets for weight and flexibility.[67] She carefully painted the faces in colors and tones that indicated how long the person had been dead and, in applicable cases, the cause of death. She knit the victim's stockings and appropriate clothes with thread that she unraveled from fabric, using needles normally used for lace making. Each doll wears undergarments.

In one photograph, Lee nimbly attends to a six-inch doll in her seemingly gigantic hand. The expression on her face is stern and concentrated, as if she were performing a delicate operation to save the tiny life, when in fact she is preparing it to replicate death. Lee wrote to her son:

> *I have been working on the bodies and have three of them done,—dressed, posed & quite definitely dead. Also, I have made several garments—long coat—plaid skirt & plain green short coat - flowered dressing gown etc.—to hang in the closet of the red bedroom. Right now I am knitting a pair of silk stockings—covering two photograph albums with velvet and making a red and green plaid umbrella.*[68]

While there is something slightly creepy about her "killing" and arranging the dolls that brings to mind the artwork of Hans Bellmer and E. T. A. Hoffmann's *The Sandman* or perhaps even the insane rituals of serial killers, the labor-intensive care and precision with which she made their clothes and painted their faces reflects a sort of attention usually described as loving. She was never satisfied with her work; instead, she complained the faces were not as realistic as she desired, and the bodies never seemed to assume or hold a satisfying position.

In creating the miniature corpses, Lee performed a kind of domestic surgery. She stuffed and attached body parts, sewed clothes, dressed the dolls, and painted their faces. Lee began with the interior and moved to the exterior, which is a reversal of the medical examiner's work, in which the body is probed from the outside in. When viewing dead bodies at crime scenes or in the morgue, Lee didn't cringe or balk. Her willingness to confront the human body in a state of abjection and decay contradicts her upbringing by parents who believed she "shouldn't know anything about the human body."[69] More in keeping with how she was raised, her reaction to dead bodies in the examination room was one of removal and detachment. In fact, she would nonchalantly eat lunch as bodies were being cut open in front of her. While it's likely Lee was drawn to the body because it was a forbidden

Using a tweezer, Frances Glessner Lee arranges the corpse of Lizzie Miller in *Dark Bathroom.*

I have no company but my doll baby and God.

FRANCES GLESSNER LEE, *age four, quoted in journal of Frances Macbeth Glessner*

territory in her childhood, when she was face to face with one, she was unable to see it in relation to herself. In this, Lee seems very like the woman Susan Griffin described in *Woman and Nature: The Roaring inside Her*:

> She is told instead she must learn to move about the human body without feeling. (She must leave feeling behind.) No one wonders if there might have been a use for that feeling—it is discarded before it is examined. She shall never know about death. The anatomy lesson becomes lifeless.

> And now this probing of the body gives us no help against our fear of death. Yet isn't that why we wanted to see the body, despite our loathing, despite our fear, because of the fear, our feeling?[70]

THORNE ROOMS

Unlikely though it may seem, another upper-class woman from Chicago constructed a series of miniatures for educational purposes.[71] Mrs. James Thorne made nearly a hundred miniature rooms that represent rooms from various historical periods—Georgian, Victorian, Greek Revival, Louis XII, and modern—in America, Europe, and Asia. The purpose of the Thorne Rooms was to expose the public to period rooms, a phenomenon that gained popularity in American museums in the 1920s.[72]

Like the Nutshell Studies, the Thorne Rooms are extraordinarily detailed and exactly proportioned on a scale of one inch to one foot. They range in subject from grandiose halls to intimate parlors. As Bruce Hatton Boyer points out in his essay "Creating the Thorne Rooms," Mrs. Thorne reproduced only the styles and periods she believed to be noteworthy; thus, the majority of the American rooms depict New England and the Old South.[73] Unlike the elegant and cultivated upper-class

Thorne Rooms, the Nutshells document a lower-middle-class domesticity normally excluded from period-room exhibits. Both women, however, preserve their social milieu: Mrs. Thorne by building interiors that memorialize and celebrate "appropriate" homes, Lee by editing upper-class homes out of the crime-scene models.

Neither Lee nor Thorne attended college, and both expressed regret about this, yet it is unlikely they would have produced their respective products had they received a formal education. Instead, both drew from the knowledge and tools with which society equipped them. Lee, however, *never* referred to the Nutshells as dollhouses, because the Nutshells were constructed for a scientific purpose, and dollhouses are either collected by women or played with by children. As an article from the *Boston Globe* stated, some people mistook Lee for "a rich eccentric indulging a compulsion to play with dolls."[74] On the other hand, although Mrs. Thorne's undertaking began with making dollhouses for children, Flora Gill Jacobs point out that this connection is deliberately ignored in the "official" literature about the rooms.[75] The dollhouse has an undesirable association because, through its intimate connection with two marginalized groups, women and children, it risks devaluing and trivializing the work of Lee and Thorne. But it is hard to resist comparing the creations of these women to the dollhouses used to socialize young girls for culturally sanctioned gender roles. Utilizing an object that prepares girls for their future role in the home, Mrs. Thorne created period rooms, which elevated the predominately feminine occupation of interior decoration to a respected art form. Lee's models are more potentially subversive. They introduce threat and danger into the roles young girls emulate while at play and present the architecture of the home as a deadly terrain where prosaic objects have a secret life as murder weapons. The monstrous acts seem all the more horrible when they are contained in the dollhouse, a domain associated with childhood and innocence.

I found a door that resembled a dollhouse door built into an adult house for no reason and behind this door there were stairs that I climbed and at the top I found myself in a larger, though not a big, room. This was the place in which I wanted to be.

KATHY ACKER, *My Mother: Demonology*

KILLING THE ANGEL IN THE HOUSE

Hanging above the hearth in *Living Room* is a painting of a peaceful house surrounded by lush green foliage. The house sits beside a dirt road lined with birch trees that leads to a distant clearing. The happy and secure house in the painting counterbalances the destroyed home.

The painting is reminiscent of a photograph that hung above the Glessners' fireplace in Chicago; it depicted Abingdon Abbey, a rural, preindustrial building that served as the prototype for H. H. Richardson's design of the house. And the painting itself is a representation of Lee's cottage on the Rocks estate. Lee made her house the symbol of the unattained ideal to which the family in *Living Room* aspired. Her carpenter surmised that she incorporated a miniature painting of her own house in a Nutshell Study "because she was so proud of it."[76]

As a product of her snobbish, well-mannered, patriarchal upbringing, Lee considered herself above the "immoral" crimes she reproduced. The models can be likened to elaborately intertwined puzzles that she put together in the safety of her home. Dominance and control are the adjectives that best characterize her relationship with the models. She tried to remain at a distance: these crimes had happened to the types of people who played roles she never assumed and lived in houses she would not deign to occupy. However, by hanging a miniature painting of her house in *Living Room*, Lee introduced an autobiographical element into the models, superfluous to the crime scene.

This was not an isolated incident, there is other evidence that personally implicates Lee in the models. In a letter to her son, John, she wrote, "I wish you could see the latest model—it's so cute. There is a kerosene stove in it copied from the little one we used to have at Camp, the chimneys and all."[77] In another letter to John she wrote, "Some of the details are quite amusing and I have my own private fun about them."[78] The model *Pink Bathroom* shares its name with a room in the Cottage. The pink bathroom in Lee's house has fish light fixtures, linking it even further to the model, which is decorated with fish wallpaper. According to one article, Lee wore a blue suit a year after it was "unfit" in order to create the properly worn material for a doll's trousers.[79] There is no telling what other details held secret meanings.

There is more than one story being told in the models. Sometimes it's hard to tell where one story ends and another begins. *Log Cabin*, for example, is a composite of actual crimes. The "Hy-Da-Way" sign on the cabin was inspired by a sign Lee saw while on a drive in New Hampshire. The cabin's structure is similar to Lee's childhood playhouse, which was itself an upscale version of a dollhouse—a small log cabin built to her size and equipped with a working stove. Designed on the Rocks estate by the Arts and Craft artist Isaac Scott, the miniature replica of a log cabin was in keeping with the Arts and Crafts ideology and was symbolic of American values such as self-sufficiency, practicality, and independence. The log cabin was also associated with Dr. Magrath: during college Lee's brother and Dr. Magrath traveled to the Rocks for winter sports, where the log cabin playhouse, according to Lee, "proved ideal for bachelor meals."[80] These connections were brought full circle when Lee began to make the crime-scene models in her little playhouse (before moving to her larger workshop in the Farm House) and later made the Nutshell

That the world of things can open itself to reveal a secret life—indeed, to reveal a set of actions and hence a narrativity and history outside the given field of perception—is a constant daydream that the miniature presents.

SUSAN STEWART, *On Longing: Narratives of the Miniature, the Gigantic, the Souvenir, the Collection*

NOW we know everything— except why the murder was actually committed.

SIGMUND FREUD

Frances Glessner Lee working on the Nutshell Studies.

Study *Log Cabin*. The autobiographical elements had nothing to do with "convicting the guilty, clearing the innocent, and finding the truth in a nutshell." They inform us that Lee was intimately involved with the models. This is our clue, our invitation to look more closely for her.

Sexual conflict was at the heart of many of the Nutshell crimes, and it's difficult not to notice that the majority of the victims are women who suffered violent deaths in the home:

> *Robin Barnes: dead on kitchen floor*
> *Kate Judson: shot in bed*
> *Linda Mae Judson: shot in crib*
> *Marie Jones: stabbed in bedroom closet*
> *Jessie Comptom: hanged in attic*
> *Rose Fishman: dead on bathroom floor*
> *Dorothy Dennison: dead on parsonage parlor floor*
> *Unknown woman: dead in bed*
> *Maggie Wilson: dead in bathtub*
> *Ruby Davis: dead on living-room stairs*
> *Annie Morrison: dead on ground below second-story porch*
> *Wilby Jenks: dead in bed*

Of the male victims, four of the corpses are represented in bed, the others are in more traditionally masculine parts of the house (the garage, the barn, at a rendezvous cabin), and one is in jail.

On the one hand, because the Nutshells depict the everyday isolation of women in the home and expose the violence that originates and is enacted there, they can be viewed as a precursor to the women's movement, which sought to eradicate the division between public and private space. On the other hand, the models can be read as replicating cultural stereotypes by depicting women as passive victims. In *Over Her Dead Body* Elisabeth Bronfen suggests that in Western culture, woman and death are both considered enigmatic and are represented as a "limit and excess."[81]

While Lee was certainly not a feminist, I am not convinced that her creation of miniature female corpses was straightforwardly assaultive and voyeuristic. Rather, I believe the models were a projection of Lee's subconscious hatred of Woman as constructed and maintained by society. Lee was terribly uncomfortable in the role that society prescribed for her as an upper-class woman. Domestic life, especially, never suited her. As we have seen, her houses were a place of refuge, personal expression, and pride, but they were also a source

of confinement, disempowerment, and anxiety; this created a perpetual push-pull. Denied a college education because "a lady didn't go to school,"[82] Lee followed the route expected of her: marriage, motherhood, and genteel domestic activities. Her marriage failed almost immediately. Although she wanted to put the whole ordeal behind her, her husband refused to grant her a divorce; a painful situation was drawn out, exasperated, and she remained her estranged husband's "property." Much can be gleaned from the fact that the sole woman in Lee's family in whom she confided and by whom she felt understood was her aunt Helen Macbeth, a musician and painter who had "surprisingly liberal" views,[83] and who never married. Supported by Mr. and Mrs. Glessner, Macbeth once declared, "I've never had a home of my own."[84] Lee also spent her life in houses that were not her own, suffering from her father's demeaning control. She wasn't given ample space or independence as a daughter to be a contented mother. Lee's own son, John, suggested that perhaps she should have "been a man, at liberty to pursue a profession."[85]

In *Differencing the Canon*, Griselda Pollock (following Julia Kristeva) explores, "not a woman artist's intent, what she is expressing because she is a woman, but rather *feminine desire* and *feminine pleasure* that can be realized only by being inscribed somewhere and somehow, masquerading (or rather passing within the conventions) and transgressive (disturbing them) at the same time."[86] Similarly, Bronfen considers women writers who use the convention of the muse and embrace death from a position between "cultural complicity and critique."[87] These formulations proved extremely helpful for my consideration of Lee's relationship to the Nutshells. While Lee was perpetuating the popular trope of the female corpse that is so pervasive in painting, film, and crime fiction, she unconsciously projected and identified herself with the miniature; each doll signified Lee's murder/suicide. The corpses in the Nutshells are all stereotypes that are externalized or mirrored in the interiors where they are depicted. We encounter a seemingly perfect housewife in *Kitchen*; the room of a prostitute (a scarlet woman) is red, and her murder suspect is Mr. Green (the complement/opposite of red); the old woman hanged in the attic is surrounded by antiquated objects; and the woman in *Dark Bathroom* was last seen drinking with "male friends." The appearance always deceives, and oftentimes the murderer has created a false solution to conceal his crime (for instance, the surface of the room implies that the old woman killed herself because she was growing old, but this inference is not to be trusted). Likewise, throughout her life, Lee was stereotyped and forced into roles that she despised, maintaining surface appearances and perhaps attempting to escape her identity by focusing on and trying to control the endless details in her life.[88]

As mentioned earlier, Lee single-handedly created the miniature corpses, and this was her main role in making the models, despite her total dissatisfaction with their appearances. She could have hired a professional doll maker, as time and money had no bearing in her production of the models. Why did she insist on making the miniature dolls herself? What did she think about when she knit the tiny stockings and executed the dolls? I think Lee's creation of mutilated female bodies reflected her own ambivalence about her sexuality and her repressed hatred of Woman. The disturbing female corpses also help us to understand the complex relationship women had to their bodies in a repressive culture where they were raised not to know anything about their bodies, and the female sex was continually held responsible for murder.

Woolf wrote, "These were the two adventures of my professional life. The first—killing the Angel in the House— I think I solved. She died. But the second, telling the truth about my own experience as a body, I do not think I solved."[89] Although Lee followed her unconscious compulsion to kill the miniature female corpses, she never came to terms with this murder. After a half century, she finally achieved fulfillment through her successful career in legal-medicine. By co-opting a feminine craft she gained respect and acceptance in a male-dominated field; by killing the angel in the house, she acquired authorship and finally began to live. However, Lee never negotiated an entirely satisfactory place for herself in

this domain, as she didn't have "letters after [her] name,"[90] and when she defended herself she wrongly tried to convince them, "I am not trying to butt in or to run anything."[91] Meanwhile, that was exactly what she was trying to do. She was conceptualized as a maternal figure, a role she promoted because it was the only one she knew, the only one available to her. She could never exist in the world the way she wanted to because home and femininity continued to haunt her.

Although Lee's self-conflict and internal turmoil are revealed in the models with frightening acuity, she never solved this personal mystery. She was close, she was verging on something, she might have even caught a glimpse of herself in the miniature deaths, but she hesitated, took a step backward, and regained composure. Once the models were installed at Harvard, the emphasis was placed on the detective (the powers of observation and the solution to the crime) and the victim disappeared. Meanwhile, Lee stood off to the side of the room, watching the burly policemen as they examined her delicate, deadly creations. She left us with the dead woman in the house.

LEFT: Frances Glessner Lee's Log Cabin Playhouse, the Rocks estate, *Bethlehem, N.H.* RIGHT: The Nutshell Study *Log Cabin.*

 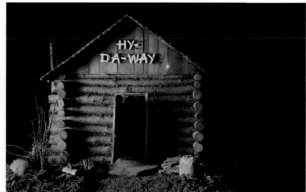

AFTERWORD: THE SWEDISH PORCH

There is one last piece of vital evidence: the *Swedish Porch*, a model constructed to replicate Lee's favorite room in her house. Lee added the Swedish porch onto her cottage just as World War II was beginning.[92] The walls were stenciled with colorful flowers and fish, and the windows faced inside to the living room and dining room. The roof was composed of hundreds of glass panes that opened individually. The Swedish porch was an in-between space that allowed Lee to exist both inside and outside. She used to sit in a rocking chair in the far right-hand corner of the porch, facing the fireplace and the outside windows. The light swimming through the ceiling splashed fanciful shadows and patterns on the walls. From this spot, she often wrote letters and ate her lunch.

Like the rocking chair where Lee used to sit, the rocking chair in the model, made according to her specifications, rocks back and forth exactly twelve times before pausing. The irregular floor tiles correspond to the shape, placement, and color of the tiles in the human-size porch. The miniature trunk is cracked in the same spot as Lee's antique trunk, and the knots on the wooden table are in exactly the same place and are proportionally the same size.

Built after she completed the Nutshell Studies of Unexplained Death, the model can be read as an act of closure, an introspective response to the crime-scene models signaling that Lee had withdrawn her attention from the outside world. Unfortunately, Lee died before the *Swedish Porch* was finished.

There is no corpse in the *Swedish Porch*, nor was it meant to contain one. Yet it is not empty—it is haunted by Lee's ghost. Her ghost is not what one ordinarily imagines a ghost to be—insubstantial, disappearing out of the corner of the eyes, solemnly waiting to avenge a wrong. Instead, Lee's ghost demands space and is undeniably present even while invisible. She laughs out loud, a laugh so powerful that the house reverberates. With anger and longing, she imagines all the lives she never lived. She imagines what it feels like to walk freely through city streets, to love passionately, to inhabit spaces differently.

I sat beside her as the last bit of afternoon light swam through the glass ceiling, and we played a game of imagining that I could be you and you could be me.

Do you see me?

Do you see me?

A woman's nature is like a great house full of rooms:
there is the hall, through which everyone passes in going in
and coming out; the drawing room,
where one receives formal visits; the sitting room,
where the members of the family come and go as they like; but beyond that,
far beyond, are other rooms, the handles of whose doors
are perhaps never turned; no one knows the way to them,
no one knows whither they lead;
and in the innermost room, holy of holies, the soul sits alone
and waits for a footstep that never comes.

EDITH WHARTON, *The Fullness of Life*

There is no body in the house at all.

SYLVIA PLATH, *The Detective*

Model of the Swedish Porch.

Notes

1. Erle Stanley Gardner, "She Would Battle for Ideas at the Drop of Her Hat," *Boston Sunday Globe*, February 4, 1962, 1–2.

2. Percy Lee, interview with Corinne Botz, Mystic, Conn., October 2001.

3. Richardson believed that windows in urban houses were "not to look out of." "You no sooner get them than you shroud them with two thickness of window shades, and then add double sets of curtains." Thus, when designing the Glessner House, he asked John Glessner, "Have you the courage to build the house without windows on the street front?" To which Glessner responded, "Yes, knowing that I could tear up the plan if I didn't like it." John Jacob Glessner, *The Story of a House* (manuscript, 1923; first published by the Chicago Architecture Foundation, 1992), 12, 23.

4. The warm interior versus the cold exterior of the house emphasized the tension between public and private, city and house, masculine and feminine. Thomas C. Hubka links the architecture of the Glessner House to the social conflicts that occurred in Chicago at that time, most important, the railroad strike (1877) and the Haymarket Riots (1886). According to Hubka, the working-class revolt threatened the upper-class sense of personal safety, causing the Glessners to seek refuge in their home. Thomas C. Hubka, "H. H. Richardson's Glessner House: A Garden in the Machine," *Winterthur Portfolio* 24, no. 4 (winter 1989): 221, 229.

5. In her journal, Mrs. Glessner recorded thirty-four comments that were made about the house when it was first built. One passerby remarked, "It looks like an old jail." Another said, "I should flee to your fort for protection in case of war." The *Chicago Evening Journal* reported, "Prairie Ave is a social street and also a gossipy one and it does not suit the neighbors that this newcomer should exclude all possibility of watching his windows and finding out what may be going on within doors." Frances Macbeth Glessner, "Journals (1879–1921)," May 4, 1887–September 19, 1887, Chicago Historical Society, Archives and Manuscript Department, 2–18.

6. George Pullman, cited in *Family Reunion* by Percy Maxim Lee and John Glessner Lee (Chicago: privately published, 1971), 340.

7. Glessner, *The Story of a House*, 3.

8. Among these were paintings and drawings that were made by "personal friends," embroideries and linen created by Mrs. Glessner and her sisters, a photograph of H. H. Richardson, and handcrafted furniture and objects. John Glessner described "a beautifully veneered mahogany work table made by my grandfather Glessner with his own hands" and an "oak silver-chest that George carved himself" and the William Morris rugs "woven especially for this house." Glessner, *The Story of a House*, 15–21.

9. Ibid., 21.

10. Joan M. Hansen, "One Family's Search for the Arts & Crafts Ideal," *Style: 1900* 12, no. 2 (spring/summer 1999): 44.

11. Frances Macbeth Glessner, "Journals," Sunday, January 23, 1889.

12. Isaac Scott, a close family friend, architect, and Arts and Craft artist, visited the Glessners' New Hampshire estate each summer and was Lee's companion (despite a great age difference). Scott taught Lee woodcarving and was an influential mentor:

    Every building had a name and a board carved with that name nailed on it and the date of its building, and it was always my job to paint these signs, the hollowed out letters in white and all the rest of our standard barn red. Mr. Scott supervised this work and would not tolerate any careless or slipshod results—if I didn't get the edges of the letters clean cut and accurate, he would wipe off the paint and I would start all over again. He was never cross or impatient but would make some scathing comment on my work, generally humorous such as "an old hen could do as well as that if she stepped in the paint and then walked across the board. Can't you do better than an old hen? You were in a hurry—never hurry—take time to do your job and do it well.

    Frances Glessner Lee, *The Lee News* (1961). This is the origin of Lee's mantra when making the crime-scene models, that time and money were irrelevant, the only important thing was that it be done well.

13. Susan Stewart, *On Longing: Narratives of the Miniature, the Gigantic, the Souvenir, the Collection* (1984; reprint, Durham, N.C.: Duke University Press, 1993), 68.

14. John Jacob Glessner, "Mrs. John J. Glessner: An Appreciation: A Little History, a Tribute," 7. The manuscript is in the collection of the Glessner House Museum, Chicago. Compliments of Glessner House Museum.

15. Pete Martin, "How Murderers Beat The Law," *Saturday Evening Post*, December 10, 1949, 53. As a benchmark of how conservative John Glessner was, a letter from his father discusses the merit of her attending school: "What is Fannie's program for the future? I have been thinking you might place her in the Chicago University, which will be a valuable school for the higher education of young ladies." Frances Macbeth Glessner, "Journals," 1893.

16. William Bentinck-Smith and Elizabeth Stouffer, *Harvard University History of Named Chairs* (Cambridge: Mass, 1991), 182.

17. Frances Glessner Lee, letter to the Advisory Board of the Frances Glessner Lee Trust, original dated June 5, 1951, Glessner House Museum, Chicago. Compliments of Glessner House Museum.

18. Virginia Woolf, *A Room of One's Own* (1929; reprint, San Diego, New York, and London: Harvest Books, 1989), 68. Reprinted by permission of the publisher.

19. Lee, *Family Reunion*, 412.

20. Ibid., 396.

21. Ibid., 259.

22. Ibid., 396.

23. Woolf, *A Room of One's Own*, 94.

24. The Glessners initially stayed at the Twin Mountain House in New Hampshire. However, with characteristic moral correctness Mr. Glessner decided "a summer hotel is not a good place to raise the children." In 1882 the Glessners bought the first one hundred acres of the Rocks estate.

25. In general, the houses and buildings adhered to the Shingle Style that was popular in New England estates at the turn of the century.

26. Frances Glessner Lee, *The Lee News* (1961), 10.

27. Lee and Lee, *Family Reunion*, 404. Lee not only lived under her parents' oppressiveness but she literally lived below them on the hill.

28. Ibid., 404.

29. Ibid., 396.

30. Lee and Lee, *Family Reunion*, 399.

31. Ibid.

32. Robert F. Bradford, "Harvard Studies Homicide: The New Models of Unexplained Death," *Harvard Alumni Bulletin*, Magnetic North 6, no. 2 (autumn 1988): 372.

33. Jürgen Thorwald, *The Century of the Detective*, translated from German by Richard and Clara Winston (New York: Harcourt, Brace & World, 1965), 201.

34. Bentinck-Smith and Stouffer, *Harvard University History of Named Chairs*, 183.

35. Frances Glessner Lee, letter to the Advisory Board of the Frances Glessner Lee Trust, 1951, Glessner House Archive, Chicago.

36. Prior to this, Dr. Magrath was a lecturer in the Harvard Medical School. Magrath's connection to the school, the fact that Lee resided in New England, and Harvard's status as an ivy-league school all influenced her decision to establish the department there. Magrath retired in 1937.

37. Bentinck-Smith and Stouffer, *Harvard University History of Named Chairs*, 182–83.

38. She endowed $250,000, almost the entire fortune she inherited from her uncle, George Blocksam Glessner, to establish the Harvard Department of Legal Medicine.

39. *Harvard Medical Alumni Bulletin*, Medical School Notes, January 1948, 35–37. Although Lee paved the way for changing the system, there remains a need for reform, as there is still a combination of Medical Examiners, Coroners, and Mixed ME and Coroner systems in the U.S.

40. This was later renamed Seminar in Homicide Investigation.

41. Frances Glessner Lee, letter to the Advisory Board of the Frances Glessner Lee Trust, 1951, Glessner House Museum, Chicago.

42. Erle Stanley Gardner, *The Case of the Dubious Bridegroom* (New York: William Morrow, 1949). Gardner dedicated the foreword to *The Case of the Dubious Bridegroom* to Lee.

43. Frances Glessner Lee, letter to the Advisory Board of the Frances Glessner Lee Trust, 1951, Glessner House Museum, Chicago. To foster informality, Lee also supplied the policemen with cigarettes and cigars. She allowed smoking because the men were not used to sitting for a long period and she wanted them to remain attentive. The label on the matches read LEGAL MEDICINE so that the officers would become "a little more familiar with the term," according to Lee.

44. Frances Glessner Lee, Foreword to the Investigator, reprinted in this volume.

45. Frances Glessner Lee, quoted in "How Murderers Beat the Law," *Saturday Evening Post*, December 10, 1949, 53.

46. Lee also received a number of other awards and honors including: honorary curator of the George Burgess Magrath Library of Legal Medicine; honorary member of the Massachusetts Medico-Legal Society; honorary member of the Maine Medico-Legal Society; charter member of the New Hampshire Medico-Legal Society; active member of the International Association of Police Chiefs; associate member of the International Association for Identification; honorary member of the New England Policewomen's Association; past president and secretary-treasurer of the Harvard Associates in Police Science; honorary captain in the Virginia State Police. Information courtesy of the Glessner House Museum, Chicago.

47. Frances Heminway, interview with Corinne Botz, Putney, Vt., May 2002.

48. Frances Glessner Lee, Citizen Fellowship acceptance speech, Institute of Medicine of Chicago.

49. Pete Martin, "How Murderers Beat the Law," *Saturday Evening Post*, December 10, 1949, 56.

50. Virginia Lee, interview with Corinne Botz, Mystic, Conn., October 2001; Percy Lee, interview with Corinne Botz, Mystic, Conn., October 2001.

51. William F. Baker, "The Nutshell Official Publication of the Harvard Associates in Police Science," June 1975, 3.

52. Frances Glessner Lee, personal letter to the Advisory Board of the Frances Glessner Lee Trust, 1951, Glessner House Museum, Chicago.

53. Frances Glessner Lee, letter to the Advisory Board of the Frances Glessner Lee Trust, 1951, Glessner House Museum, Chicago.

54. Charles L. Banino, quoted in "She Invested a Fortune in Police, Entertained Them Royally at Ritz," *Boston Sunday Globe*, February 4, 1962, 46.

55. William F. Baker, interview with Corinne Botz, Columbia, Md., spring 1999.

56. Lee and Lee, *Family Reunion*, 409.

57. Henry C. Lee, Timothy Palmbach, Marilyn T. Miller, *Henry Lee's Crime Scene Handbook* (Academic Press, 2001), xi.

58. Alton Mosher worked for Lee until her death. While working for her, the Moshers were provided with a house at the Rocks.

59. Frances Glessner Lee, "Foreword to the Investigator," reproduced in this volume.

60. Frances Glessner Lee, ad for Profitable Hobbies, Kansas City.

61. Gaston Bachelard, *The Poetics of Space*, trans. Maria Jolas (Boston: Beacon Press, 1994), 150.

62. Frances Glessner Lee, factual corrections, Harvard Medical School, Department of Legal Medicine Records, February 25, 1950. Francis A. Countway Library of Medicine, Boston, Mass.

63. Frances Glessner Lee, letter to Cranford Miniatures, 1948, Glessner House Museum, Chicago.

64. In 1916 A. H. Davenport merged with Irving & Casson.

65. Frances Glessner Lee, letter to Irving & Casson—A. H. Davenport Company, 1944. Glessner House Museum, Chicago. Compliments of Glessner House Museum.

66. Frances Glessner Lee, letter to Cranford Miniatures, 1948, Glessner House Museum, Chicago.

67. Richard F. Dempewolff, "Mysterious Death Their Business," *Popular Mechanics* 100, no. 1 (July 1953): 240.

68. Frances Glessner Lee, letter to John Lee, September 28, 1944. Courtesy of the Glessner family.

69. Frances Glessner Lee, quoted in "How Murderers Beat the Law," *Saturday Evening Post*, December 10, 1949, 53.

70. Susan Griffin, *Woman and Nature: The Roaring inside Her* (San Francisco: Sierra Club Books, 2000).

71. I am grateful to Virginia Lee for bringing to my attention the Thorne Room.

72. Kathleen Culbert-Aguilar and Michael Abramson, photographers, *Miniature Rooms: The Thorne Rooms at the Art Institute of Chicago* (New York: Abbeville Press, 1983), 12.

73. Bruce Hatton Boyer, "Creating the Thorne Rooms," in *Miniature Rooms*, 15.

74. Earl Banner, "She Invested a Fortune in Police, Entertained Them Royally at Ritz" *Boston Sunday Globe*, February 4, 1962, 46.

75. Flora Gill Jacobs, *A History of Dolls' Houses* (New York: Charles Scribner's Sons, 1953), 296.

76. Alton Mosher, interview with Corinne Botz, Salem, N.H., June 2002.

77. Frances Glessner Lee, letter to John Lee, December 28, 1943. Courtesy of the Glessner family.

78. Frances Glessner Lee, letter to John Lee, February 11, 1945. Courtesy of the Glessner family.

79. "The Nutshell Murders of Mrs. Frances Lee," *Harvard Alumni Bulletin* (summer 1961), 23.

80. Frances Glessner Lee, handwritten notes for "Yankee Yarns" radio program, Glessner House Museum, Chicago. Compliments of Glessner House Museum.

81. Elisabeth Bronfen, *Over Her Dead Body: Death, Femininity and the Aesthetic* (New York: Routledge, 1992), 205.

82. Frances Glessner Lee, quoted in Pete Martin, "How Murderers Beat the Law," 53.

83. Lee and Lee, *Family Reunion*, 302.

84. Ibid.

85. Ibid., 412.

86. Griselda Pollock, *Differencing the Canon: Feminist Desire and the Writing of Art's Histories*, 146.

87. Bronfen proposes that "the death these authors write can only be defined ex negativo. It is not the death of the other, or death as Other. Rather it remains somehow within this representational system. The feminine subject position writing out of death is still a position of oscillation with no defined or fixed place, but here somehow within." Bronfen, *Over Her Dead Body*, 395.

88. As Erle Stanley Gardner put it, "I don't believe she has ever overlooked a detail in her life." Gardner, *The Case of the Dubious Bridegroom*, Foreword. Once, Lee chided her cook for adding lemon to a dish. The cook replied that there certainly was no lemon in the dish. But Lee insisted otherwise. The cook eventually recalled squeezing a lemon early that morning, the faintest residue of which was still on her hands and had been transferred to Lee's dish. Another revealing story: fish objects and oriental vases lined the shelves around Lee's living room. There was a number on the bottom of each object that corresponded to a number on the shelf where it was meant to rest. The objects were dusted daily. Every morning Lee walked by the shelf and straightened the objects that were slightly askew, deeming the housemen incompetent under her breath.

89. Woolf, quoted in Bronfen, *Over Her Dead Body*, 395.

90. Frances Glessner Lee, letter to the Advisory Board of the Frances Glessner Lee Trust, 1951.

91. Frances Glessner Lee, quoted in "How Murderers Beat the Law," 53.

92. Ralph Mosher was a carpenter who helped build the porch. Recognizing his skill and precision, she asked Ralph, when the porch was completed, if he would like to work full-time on the models. As mentioned, after Ralph's death his position was passed on to his son, Alton. Alton built the model of the *Swedish Porch*; thus the story of the carpenters is brought full circle. It also creates a marker in Lee's life for the models.

12

INVESTIGATOR

The Nutshell models are built on the scale of one inch to one foot. Because continuous action cannot be represented, each model is a tableau depicting the scene at the most effective moment, very much as if a motion picture were stopped at such a point. The inspector may best examine them by imagining himself a trifle less than six inches tall. With that firmly in mind, a few moments of observation will then make him able to step into the scene and there find many tiny details that might otherwise escape notice. Comparison with certain familiar objects will also be helpful, as for instance, a table of standard height (30) inches becomes 2 1/2 inches—an ordinary side chair with seat 18 inches high is now only 1 1/2 inches high—a revolver of about 11 1/4 inches overall length here but a scant inch, et cetera.

In presenting these cases the Nutshell laboratories are acting as a consulting agency, the time and date when a case is presented to them is not necessarily the same as the time and date when it is reported to the police. Each case is based on actual facts, altered to avoid identification and enlarged to create a more intricate problem.

It will simplify the examiner's work if he will first choose the point at which he enters the scene and, beginning at his left at the place, describe the premises in a clockwise direction back to the starting point, thence to the center of the scene and ending with the body and its immediate surroundings. He should look for and record indications of the social and financial status of the people involved in each model as well as anything that may illustrate their state of mind up to or at the time of demonstration. Unless otherwise indicated, no photographs or fingerprints will be available—the investigator must base his report on the material as represented. The observer should approach his assignment as if he were the special officer detailed to investigate the case. The information supplied concerning each model is that which the officer would normally have when sent to investigate, together with the first statements obtained from one or more of the most immediate accessible witnesses. It must not be overlooked that these statements may be true, mistaken, or intentionally false, or a combination of any two or all three of these. The observer must therefore view each case with an entirely open mind. The Nutshell Studies are not presented as crimes to be solved—they are, rather, designed as exercises in observing and evaluating indirect evidence, especially that which may have medical importance. The investigator must bear in mind that he has a twofold responsibility—to clear the innocent as well as to expose the guilty. He is seeking only the facts—the Truth in a Nutshell.

Three-Room Dwelling

ROBERT JUDSON
foreman in a shoe factory; his wife,
KATE JUDSON
and their baby,
LINDA MAE JUDSON
dead

REPORTED
MONDAY, NOVEMBER

PAUL AND SARAH ABBOTT
neighbors, questioned

PAUL ABBOTT'S STATEMENT

Bob Judson and I drove to work together,

alternating cars. It was my week to drive. I arrived at his house a few minutes late—about 7:35 A.M., I blew the horn a few times and when he didn't come out I went to the factory thinking he would come in his own car.

SARAH ABBOTT'S STATEMENT

After Paul left I watched for Bob to come out.

Finally about 8:15 A.M., seeing no signs of activity at the Judson house, I went over to their porch and tried the front door. It was locked. I knocked and called but got no answer. Then I walked around to the kitchen porch, but that door was also locked. I looked in through the glass, saw some blood and ran home and called the police.

The model shows the premises just before Sarah Abbott went to the house. N.B.: Sunrise at 6:17 A.M. weather clear. No lights were lighted in the house. Both outside doors were locked on the inside.

FRONT PORCH

1 **FRONT PORCH.** The exterior of the house is exceedingly harmonious and respectable. This is suggestive of the evil that can lurk behind a public facade. It is reminiscent of the opening scene of David Lynch's *Blue Velvet*, in which an idyllic small town suddenly becomes deadly.

KITCHEN

2 **FOOD.** An assortment of mass-produced, processed food is proudly displayed on the kitchen shelf. While not gourmet products, they indicate pleasure in consumption, abundance, and the upward mobility of the Judson family.

3 **APPLIANCES.** The kitchen is equipped with a toaster, blender, coffeemaker, masher, sieve, and egg-beater. Labor- and time-saving devices such as these were advocated by Christine Frederick, who led the "scientific management" of the household in early-twentieth-century America. Frederick analyzed every step that a housewife took to complete a task, in order to increase efficiency and management of the household.

4 **KITCHEN TABLE.** The table is set for breakfast, evidence that Kate Judson was an organized housewife, and nothing deterred her from her customary habits on the night of October 31, 1937. She planned to wake up the next morning.

5 **RIFLE.** The investigators would: (1) check the firearm and ammunition components for latent fingerprints, (2) test-fire the gun with the box of ammunition on the kitchen shelf, (3) compare the "rifling" marks (the unique pattern of marks that are made on the bullet as it goes through the barrel) on the test-fired bullets with those found at the crime scene, (4) swab the hands of potential suspects for the presence of gunshot residue (GSR).

6 **SITTING AREA.** The kitchen is a multipurpose room that also serves as a dining and sitting area. As Daphne Spain points out in *Gendered Spaces*, the growing trend for integrated rooms in the twentieth century reflected increasing democracy in the family and the improved status of women in society.[1] While integrated, the masculine and feminine remain strictly demarcated in the sitting area: Robert Judson sat in the large easy chair and read the newspaper (connecting him to the public sphere and business), and Kate Judson sat in a petite rocking chair and read the Sears, Roebuck catalog (shopping for home products).

MASTER BEDROOM

7 **BLOOD TRAIL.** The investigators would examine the blood trail. The droplets of blood observed on the floor can indicate the speed at which the suspect was moving and the height at which the droplets originated. The bloodstains may also reveal footwear impression, drag marks, and transfer patterns.

8 **BLUE AND PINK.** A blue and pink color scheme is repeated throughout the master bedroom and baby's room. Dressed in blue pajamas, Robert Judson lies on top of the blue comforter on the floor. Kate Judson wears a pink nightgown and is covered with a pink blanket in bed. The masculine and feminine roles are clearly delineated.

9 **KATE JUDSON.** By examining trajectory and blood spatter patterns, investigators would be able to determine the position of the person who fired the shotgun.

BABY'S ROOM

10 **CARTRIDGE CASING.** The investigators would: (1) photograph the cartridge casing where it was found, (2) recover the cartridge casing, (3) determine what caliber shotgun it came from and see if it matches the shotgun on the scene, and (4) process it for latent fingerprints.

11 **DOLL.** "The doll is not only her double; it is also her child. These two functions do not exclude each other, inasmuch as the real child is also an alter ego for her mother.... She confides in her doll, she brings it up, exercises upon it her sovereign authority, sometimes even tears off its arms, beats it, tortures it. Which is to say, she experiences subjective affirmation and identification through the doll."
—Simone de Beauvoir, *The Second Sex*

12 **OVERTURNED CHAIRS.** There always seems to be an overturned chair at the scene of a crime. A chair is knocked over in the Judsons' bedroom and in Linda Mae's room. On top of Linda Mae's dresser are two miniature gold chairs, which are similarly overturned. This is a microcosm inside a microcosm.

1. Daphne Spain, *Gendered Spaces* (Chapel Hill, N.C.: University of North Carolina Press, 1992), 122–40.

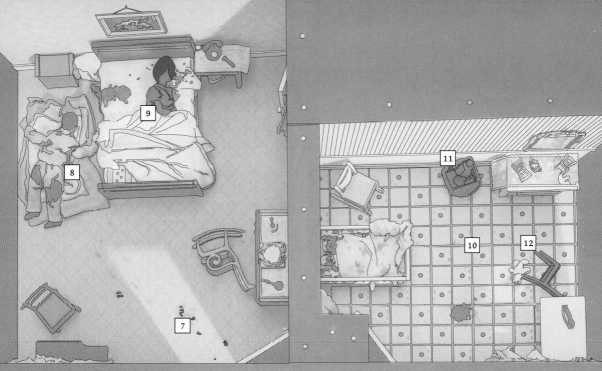

Log Cabin

ARTHUR ROBERTS
local insurance salesman, dead

MARIAN CHASE
questioned

REPORTED
THURSDAY, OCTOBER 22, 1942

MARIAN CHASE'S STATEMENT

I met Arthur at the Log Cabin on Wednesday, October 21, 1942, at about 5:00 P.M. We were having an affair.

He was married and living with his wife. I'm also married but I don't live with my husband. He told me at this meeting that the affair between us was over. We didn't quarrel. We were standing at the foot of the bunk, he turned towards the door, took a pack of cigarettes from his outside pocket, selected a cigarette, but dropped it. As he stooped over to pick it up I heard a shot—he fell flat—a gun dropped beside him. I picked up the gun and then put it back. I ran out the door, jumped in my car and drove to the police station.

The gun was identified as belonging to Arthur Roberts. Mrs. Chase identified the handbag on the bunk as belonging to her. A single bullet had passed entirely through Mr. Robert's chest from front to back and the powder around the entrance hole indicated that it had been fired at a fairly close range. The model shows the premises just after Marian Chase left and before her return with the police officer.

"My own interest in crime detection is not so much from the angle of bringing criminals to justice as it is in establishing scientifically the true facts of the case so that no innocent man is railroaded by incomplete or misleading evidence into paying for a crime he never committed."

—*Frances Glessner Lee*

HY-DA-WAY. While traveling down Route 3 Lee saw the name HY-DA-WAY on a barn, and according to her carpenter she "fell in love" with the name.[2] This inspired her to dub *Log Cabin* HY-DA-WAY. The sign was assembled from thin birch branches.

2 BRANCHES. To build *Log Cabin*, sticks were collected in the woods, cut to size, and crossed. Moss was placed inside the crevices and a rock step of a predefined shape and size was found. The tarpaper was secured by tar grooves and nails the size of a pinhead.

LOG CABIN. As a young girl, Lee had an upscale version of a dollhouse—a small house built to her size. Designed on the Rocks estate by the Arts and Craft artist Isaac Scott, it was a miniature replica of a log cabin, equipped with a working stove. There, Lee jarred jams and preserves, cooked,

and cleaned inside (for a number of years she made preserves for the entire family). She also made meals for convalescent patients with special dietary needs, an activity that resulted in her assisting local doctors in operations, then performed in patients' homes. Lastly, her small house was associated with Dr. Magrath, for during college Lee's brother and Magrath traveled to the Rocks for winter sports, where the log cabin playhouse, according to Lee, "proved ideal for bachelor meals."[3] These connections were brought full circle when Lee began to make the crime-scene models in her little playhouse (before moving to her larger workshop in the Farm House). Her log cabin playhouse is similar to the model *Log Cabin*.

4 BULLET. It took investigators three days to locate the bullet. Do you see it?

5 PURSE. In response to Marian Chase's claim that there was no quarrel, Gordon K. Carew, a detective with the Baltimore Police Department, counters, "I wouldn't believe there was no argument when they were breaking up…. there's always an argument of some kind." Carew notes, "Her purse is on the bed. His hat came off his head.

It's like they were starting to leave or just got there…. She probably shot him while he was getting the cigarette and ready to leave."

6 GUN. Why would Marian Chase pick up the gun? The firearm should be processed for latent fingerprints. While Marian Chase admits to having handled the weapon, her prints should not be located on the ammunition or ammunition components.

7 GUN LOCATION. If Arthur Roberts bent over and shot himself, as Marian Chase claims, he would have likely fallen on top of the weapon. Marian Chase's statement that the gun fell beside him is suspect.

2. Alton Mosher, interview with Corinne Botz, Salem, N.H., June 2002.

3. Frances Glessner Lee, handwritten notes for "Yankee Yarns" radio broadcast, Glessner House Museum, Chicago.

Blue Bedroom

CHARLES LOGAN
employee in box factory, dead

CAROLINE LOGAN
wife, questioned

REPORTED
NOVEMBER 3, 1943

CAROLINE LOGAN'S STATEMENT

On Tuesday night November 2nd, I was alone in the house when Charles came home about midnight. He was typically drunk and quarrelsome.

We had an argument but I finally persuaded him to go upstairs to bed. I waited downstairs for him to go to sleep before I went to bed. After about half an hour I heard him moving around and then there was a shot. I ran upstairs and found him dead.

The model illustrates the scene as found by Caroline Logan.

Blue Bedroom

 STROP. Hanging on the wall is a leather strop, used for sharpening a razor.

ELEPHANT. The elephant is a symbol of wisdom and good luck.

ROMANCE MAGAZINES. A pile of magazines on the floor includes *Love*, *Rangeland Romances*, *Screen Romances*, and *American Amateur*. One headline reads, "Hollywood's Most Beautiful Models Photographed" (Lee pasted this over the existing headline). We learn Caroline Logan's reading taste and can induce that she spent time (perhaps, contrary to her statement, that evening) in her husband's bedroom.

BOX FACTORY. Lights from the box factory where Charles Logan worked are visible through the window. This is clearly a workers' lodging: the room is unkempt, the shades are falling, and the furniture is worn.

POSTCARD. The postcard is of the Old Man of the Mountain, located in Franconia Notch, New Hampshire. It was an emblem of the State of New Hampshire that attracted millions of tourists. The mountain collapsed on Saturday, May 3, 2003, at approximately 7:30 A.M.

6 **STRING**. There is string on the bedroom dresser and string wrapped around the firearm. This is occasionally seen when an individual's arms cannot reach the trigger. The string is wrapped around the trigger or hammer and it is yanked when he or she is ready to fire the weapon.

7 **BED**. Why did Caroline and Charles Logan sleep in different bedrooms? This may be an indication of a strained relationship; on the other hand, they may be old-fashioned, or perhaps Charles Logan snored. The investigators would question Caroline Logan about this matter.

8 **IN-PLAIN-SIGHT CLUE**. There is a major in-plain-sight clue.

9 **BLOOD SPATTER**. A blood spatter examiner might be called to the scene to evaluate the bloodstain pattern on the headboard. This could reveal information about the victim's position at his time of death.

10 **GUN**. The location of the firearm is suspicious. Charles Logan is positioned on his right side, yet the firearm is on the floor behind him.

11 **BLUE TROUSERS**. Lee wore a blue suit a year after it was "unfit" in order to create the properly worn

material for a doll's trousers.

12 **CHARLES LOGAN**. The medical examiner would determine where Mr. Logan had been shot. Considering the length of the rifle, the location of Charles Logan's injuries may not be consistent with a self-inflicted wound.

Dark Bathroom

MAGGIE WILSON
dead

LIZZIE MILLER
questioned

REPORTED
November 6, 1896, by Sergeant Moriarty
of the Central City Police

LIZZIE MILLER'S STATEMENT

I roomed in the same house as Maggie, but we only spoke when we met in the hall.

I think she was subject to fits (seizures). A couple of male friends came to see her fairly regularly. Tonight, the men were in her room and there seemed to be a good deal of drinking going on. Sometime after they left, I heard the water still running in the bathroom, so I opened the door and found Maggie dead in the tub with water pouring down on her face.

The model shows the scene as discovered by Lizzie Miller.

1 TOILET PAPER. A precursor to toilet paper rolls, this precut square toilet paper was very rough and was sold by the box.

2 BATHTUB AND SINK. Investigators would process the interior and the exterior of the bathtub, sink, faucets, and spigots for latent fingerprints. While it is possible that Maggie Wilson, feeling unwell from either alcohol or illness, sat on the side of the tub and splashed cold water on her face before slipping backwards, it is far more likely that an effort to refresh oneself would occur at the sink. The presence of a rag in the basin may provide evidence of a revival effort, either by Maggie Wilson or a second party. This rag should be collected as possible evidence; investigators today would examine it to see if it contained victim or suspect DNA. The practice of placing an unconscious individual in a tub filled with cold water is a revival technique commonly employed by drug users. It seems more likely that Maggie Wilson's friends placed her in the tub and allowed the cold water to run over her face in the attempt to awaken her.

3 DROWNING IN THE BATHTUB. A landmark case with which Lee was familiar, and which may have in part inspired *Dark Bathroom*, involved a series of bathroom murders in England. Investigators were certain that a man by the name of George Joseph Smith (who used numerous aliases) was responsible for marrying three women whom he drowned shortly afterward, in order to collect his inheritance. Much to the bewilderment of investigators, there were absolutely no marks of violence on the victims.

One of the victims was epileptic and it was supposed that she drowned during a fit. However, her head was found underwater, her legs were extended and her feet were above the water. This was an impossible position for the woman to get into if she suffered a fit, since the bathtub was smaller in length than she. These facts sparked the following theory, as Jürgen Thorwald explained: "[Smith]—pretending to be engaged in a lover's teasing—might have seized the unsuspecting woman by the feet and abruptly drawn them up above the lower rim of the tub, toward himself. The upper part of his victim's body would slide underwater, and the sudden entrance of water into the nose and throat might cause a shock and sudden loss of consciousness. This would explain the absence of injuries and the minimal signs of drowning and asphyxia."[4] Their hypothesis was tested and proved correct. Smith was hanged on June 30, 1915.

This case was extremely significant in terms of forensic medicine because it related to discoveries that scientists were making about the body's nervous regulations, and reflexes that could result in death.[5]

4 BLACK STOCKINGS. Lee knit the stockings with needles the size of ordinary straight pins, a task so arduous she could only complete a few rows at a time. In a letter to her son she wrote, "Today I finished the final black cotton stocking which has been such a bore and such a job."[6]

5 LEGS. Maggie Wilson's legs are not hanging over but sticking out from the edge of the tub in an unnatural manner, indicating that the body might have been moved after rigor mortis set in. The investigators would search for a second crime scene, where the assault occurred. There might be more evidence where the crime originated, including hair, blood, a murder weapon, and so on.

One of the cases on which Lee likely based *Dark Bathroom* was a murder that Dr. Magrath investigated: the case of Marguerita Isabelle Stewart, who was found dead off a road in Concord, Massachusetts, on March 30, 1927. The *Boston Evening American* reported: "Silken-clad knees were high under her chin—and this was so important in Doctor Magrath's testimony later—the girl was found to have been bludgeoned to death, with two horrible holes in her head."[7] Frederick H. Knowlton, who was having an affair with Stewart, was apprehended. The investigation uncovered that Knowlton kept Marguerita's body in the rumble seat of his Chrysler while he ate dinner with his wife and children. He didn't dispose of her body until later on that night. According to the *Boston Evening American*, "Rigor mortis had set in while the girl was crammed into the position in which she was found, indicating that she had been stuffed into a small, narrow compartment. Lividity of the body, the coloration after death, indicated that she had been laying after death on her left side for an extended period. This was determined by marks left by the blood coagulation setting to that side through gravity. Death was due to jagged head wounds."[8] Knowlton was put to death in the electric chair.

6 MAGGIE WILSON. Through autopsy, investigators would hope to determine if the manner of Maggie Wilson's death was natural (i.e., the result of a seizure-related disorder), accidental (drowning from water being run over her face in a revival attempt), or homicide (an intentional drowning). Forensic toxicological analyses performed on blood and other body fluids would reveal blood alcohol levels and the presence of other controlled dangerous substances. These analyses would also detect those medications Maggie Wilson was taking at the time of her death, including those prescribed

for her seizure disorder. Examination of the lungs would reveal whether or not Maggie Wilson drowned. Routine samples would also be collected at autopsy, such as victim's blood, hair, and fingernails in the event suspect

4. Jürgen Thorwald, *The Century of the Detective*, translated from the German by Richard and Clara Winston (New York: Harcourt, Brace & World, 1965), 199. © 1964 by Droemersche Verlagstalt A.G. Zurich, © 1965 by Jürgen Thorwald, reprinted by permission of Harcourt, Inc.

6. Frances Glessner Lee, letter to John Lee, December 28, 1943.

7. George W. Clarke, "Take the Stand, Dr. Magrath: How Hathaway Was Convicted," *Boston Evening American*, December 14, 1938, 17.

8. Ibid.

Burned Cabin

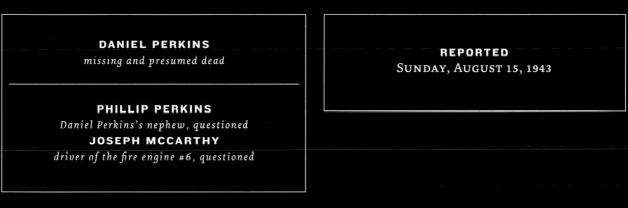

DANIEL PERKINS
missing and presumed dead

PHILLIP PERKINS
Daniel Perkins's nephew, questioned
JOSEPH MCCARTHY
driver of the fire engine #6, questioned

REPORTED
Sunday, August 15, 1943

PHILLIP PERKINS'S STATEMENT

On Saturday evening [August 14, 1943], I came to spend the night with my uncle, as I often do.

In the middle of the night the smell of smoke woke me up and I ran outside to find the house on fire and fire engines arriving. It was really confusing and I can't remember any other details.

JOSEPH MCCARTHY'S STATEMENT

The call to the fire was received at 1:30 A.M., August 15th.

We arrived and quickly extinguished the fire before the building was completely destroyed. I noticed Phillip Perkins fully clothed wandering around near the house.

The model represents the premises after the fire was extinguished and before the investigation was started or any part of the premises disturbed.

> "If a house burns down, it's gone, but the place—the picture of it—stays, and not just in my rememory, but out there in the world."
> —Toni Morrison, *Beloved*

1 **FUEL CAN.** Most individuals do not keep fuel cans in their kitchens. The residence appears to be relatively neat and uncluttered, making the location of this can additionally suspicious. The can has not likely occupied this position for very long, as it obstructs the doorway and would have created a nuisance. Crime-scene investigators should collect a sample of the can's contents and subsequently process it for latent fingerprints.

2 **BREAD AND SOUP.** Bread and soup are on the kitchen table, as if Daniel and Phillip Perkins were getting ready to eat, as opposed to having already gone to bed. This raises questions regarding the statement Phillip provided to investigators. The investigators would find out if it was customary for them to leave their food out after dinner. Perhaps there was an altercation around dinnertime and the nephew, unintentionally or purposely, killed the uncle and later started a fire to conceal his crime.

3 **BURNED CABIN.** The model was meticulously built and then meticulously burned with a blowtorch to look exactly like the building on which it was based.

4 **THE BED.** The fire was confined to the bed and adjacent bedroom wall. There is no evidence of burning on the floor, making it appear that the fire started in the bed and traveled upward toward the ceiling. Not even the fabric of the nearby chair cushion was ignited. The fire also appears to have burned more intensely at the head of the bed, as evidenced by significant charring of the headboard and adjacent wall. The bed's footboard shows differential degrees of burning. Burned and unburned samples of the bedding, bed frame, and wall should be collected and tested for the presence of accelerants.

5 **CORPSE.** The body located in the bed may or may not be that of Daniel Perkins. Mr. Perkins could be attempting to stage his death in the hopes of creating a new identity. Identification of the deceased, and the cause and manner of his death, are questions that will be answered by the medical examiner by performing an autopsy. It may be necessary to resort to dental records to confirm the identity of the deceased. In cases of extreme damage to the dental arcade, the assistance of a forensic odontologist may be necessary. The presence of soot in the trachea would indicate the victim was alive at the time of the fire and inhaled smoke. The absence of soot supports the supposition that Daniel Perkins was not alive at the time of the fire.

ANALYSES

If I were dispatched to this fatal fire scene, I would be suspicious of an arson/homicide for following reasons: Phillip Perkins claims he was awoken by the smell of smoke and ran outside to find his uncle's house ablaze. Unless Phillip sleeps in his clothes or took the time to change his clothes before exiting the house, emergency response units should not have found him wandering around the scene fully dressed. Fire investigators or crime-scene personnel should collect this clothing and swab Phillip's hands for the presence of accelerants.… The victim is still located in the bed. I cannot help to wonder why he was not located on the floor or in a position suggesting he attempted to flee his burning bed. Autopsy will determine whether the decedent had sustained injuries (fatal or incapacitating) prior to the burning episode.

DANA KOLLMANN
CRIME-SCENE INVESTIGATOR

Unpapered Bedroom

UNKNOWN WOMAN *dead*	**REPORTED** Monday, June 4, 1949
MRS. BESSIE COLLINS *landlord of rooming house, questioned*	

BESSIE COLLINS'S STATEMENT

I keep a rooming house. On Saturday, in the early afternoon, the woman who died and a man rented a room until Monday morning,

registering as Mr. and Mrs. John Smith. On Monday morning June 4th, the man left early: about 6:30 A.M. He paid for the room up until 6:00 that evening and said not to disturb his wife, because she wanted to sleep late.

About 3:00 on Monday, I told Stella Walsh, the maid, to try to get into her room to make it up. Just before 5:00, Stella told me there was something wrong. She tried twice but couldn't wake the woman. The door was not locked so Stella and I went into the room and found the woman was cold, apparently dead. We left the room without disturbing anything, locked the door behind us and kept the key. We notified the nearest patrolman.

The model shows the conditions in the room as the two women found them,

"Because they are so familiar, so evident, we are culturally blind to the ubiquity of representations of feminine death."
—Elisabeth Bronfen, *Over Her Dead Body: Death, Femininity and the Aesthetic*

1 **TRASH**. Investigators would search the contents of the trash can for indications of the identity of the decedent and her male friend.

PILLBOX. Inside the pillbox are ten capsules of the barbiturate, or "downer," Seconal. An overdose of this drug can be fatal. Combining Seconal with alcohol is extremely dangerous. The investigators would want to find out if this caused the woman's death.

3 **PILLOW**. There is lipstick on the underside of the pillow. Most women remove their makeup, particularly lipstick, prior to going to sleep. Possibly the victim was incapacitated to some degree and went to bed with her lipstick on.

CALENDAR. Every model, with the exception of *Unpapered Bedroom*, has a calendar that precisely marks the time of death. This case was reported on June 4, 1949, but the calendar on the wall is dated December 1944. No one has bothered to change the calendar for five years!

5 **WORN DOORWAY**. The rug and floor near the doorway are worn from overuse, the paint on the wall is unevenly coated, the window shade is tattered, and the bed frame is cheap (note wheels on bottom). All of these details reflect the unkempt state of the second-rate rooming house.

6 **HIGH HEELS**. The "New Look," which was introduced by Christian Dior in 1947, marked a post-war return to femininity. High-heeled shoes, cinched-waist jackets, and full skirts were popular. These are fashionable high-heeled shoes with a strap around the ankle. The green-blue heel matches the color of the woman's jacket.

7 **JANE DOE**. This case presents two problems—who was this woman? And what caused her death? These are questions that can be answered by the medical examiner through autopsy. Today, the deceased would be fingerprinted and her prints entered into a computer database. Individuals who have been arrested, work with children, operate taxicabs, or have served in the military are among those whose prints are on file. Aside from obvious trauma, the cause and manner of death may be revealed through toxicological findings, microscopic analyses, biological cultures, etc. Since Seconal tablets were found at the scene, the medical examiner would be sure to test the victim's blood for levels of this drug, as well as other controlled dangerous substances and alcohol. Oral, anal, and vaginal swabs, as well as nail clippings and hair samples (head and pubic), would be collected in the event the case is ruled a homicide and a suspect is developed at a later date.

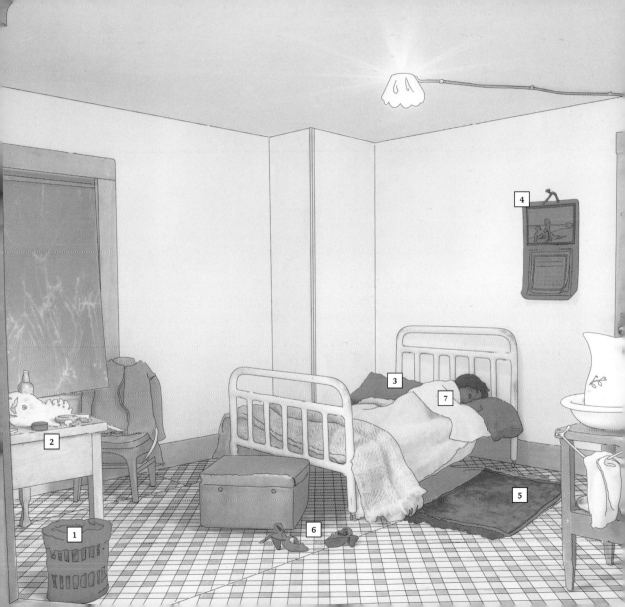

Pink Bathroom

MRS. ROSE FISHMAN

widow, dead

SAMUEL WIESS

janitor, questioned

REPORTED

TUESDAY, MARCH 31, 1942

SAMUEL WIESS'S STATEMENT

Several tenants complained of an odor and on March 30th, I began looking for what was causing the smell.

Mrs. Fishman didn't answer her bell when I rang it. I checked with the other tenants and found that she hadn't been seen recently. I then looked into her mailbox and discovered that her mail had accumulated for several days. I entered her apartment and found it in order but the odor was very strong. The bathroom door was closed. I tried to open the door but could only get it opened a little bit. The odor was much stronger around there. I immediately went downstairs and climbed the fire escape, entered the bathroom through the window, and once inside, I found Mrs. Fishman dead. I can't remember if the window was opened or closed.

The model shows the premises as Samuel Wiess found them.

1 **PINK BATHROOM.** Lee named one of the rooms in her cottage Pink Bathroom. The pink bathroom in Lee's house had a pink sink and bathtub, and fish light fixtures (she collected fish imagery), linking it to the fish wallpaper in the model. Her grandson, Hamilton Lee, postulates that fish represented "fluidity and beauty" to Lee.

2 **FISH WALLPAPER.** The wallpaper in the models does more than provide a background to the deaths: each wallpaper is oddly connected to the nature of the crimes. The underwater wallpaper gives *Pink Bathroom* the aura of a fishbowl. Water is often associated with a dream state and the unconscious. Is Rose Fishman symbolically living with the fish, weeds, coral, and reef, safe from a life she could no longer bear?

3 **MIRROR.** The three mirrors in this scene, taken together with the fish wallpaper, play with the notion of surface and depth, exterior and interior, visible and invisible. Rose Fishman's corpse is uncannily doubled in the mirror. Did she commit suicide while looking at her reflection? Did she kill herself because she was growing old and was afraid of remaining a widow? Was she an exhibitionist in want of a witness (she is in the direct sightline of the building across the street)?

4 **WINDOW.** Samuel Wiess stated that he could not remember if he found the window opened or closed. If the window had been open, it would have ventilated the bathroom and dissipated the odor of the decomposing body. It is likely that this window was closed.

5 **VANITY MIRROR.** "The woman, knowing herself, making an object of herself, believes that she is really able to see herself in the mirror.... Bored with household chores, she has the spare time to dream up her own face."
—Simone de Beauvoir, *The Second Sex*

6 **POWDER PUFF, PERFUME, AND DOILY.**
"The contemporary bathroom thus owes much of its utility to one of the great shifts shaping the late twentieth century, our growing preoccupation with our own bodies and their odours, as well as the bodies of others. No longer just a space set apart for the unsocial acts of elimination and washing, the bathroom has become a private space to cleanse the body for personal pleasure and social presentation."
—Peter Ward, *A History of Domestic Space: Privacy and the Canadian Home*

7 **BATHROOM DOOR.** The bathroom door was closed. Since Rose Fishman lived alone, it is somewhat odd that she would close the door to bathe or over the side of the tub suggests that Rose Fishman did not bathe, despite the fact that she was dressed in a bathrobe. The tub also appears to be dry. Perhaps Mrs. Fishman was looking in the mirror affixed to the back of the door.

8 **STOOL.** In Rose Fishman's pristine bathroom, the presence and location of a stool are a bit odd. Was Mrs. Fishman attempting to change a light bulb or access something above her reach?

9 **SLIPPERS.** Nothing is disturbed in the bathroom and there does not appear to have been a struggle. Even the slippers were carefully removed and conscientiously arranged on the rug.

10 **ROSE FISHMAN.** The body is in the early stage of decomposition: there is skin discoloration and slippage, the body is bloated, and purge fluids (the reddish brown discharge) are coming out of the nose and mouth. The absence of insects provides further evidence that the bathroom window was closed.

It is ironic that in this vain and pristine bathroom, which looks as if it smells of perfume, the body was discovered because of its foul odor. Perhaps to reinforce this contradiction, Lee named the victim Rose Fishman.

Attic

MISS JESSIE COMPTOM
dead

MR. HARRY FRASIER
milk deliveryman, questioned

REPORTED
TUESDAY, DECEMBER 24, 1946

HARRY FRASIER'S STATEMENT

About 6:00 this morning I stopped at Miss Comptom's kitchen door to deliver the milk.

It was really cold and I was surprised to find the door open. I put my head inside and called but no one answered so I went in to see if anything was wrong. There seemed to be nobody home. After looking through the house, I went partly up the attic stairs and saw Miss Comptom's body hanging there. I went downstairs and telephoned the police.

The policeman John T. Adams received the telephone call at 6:43 Tuesday morning, December 24, and went at once to Miss Comptom's house. The snow on the path to the kitchen door was somewhat trampled and no noticeable footprints could be recognized. There were unwashed dishes for one person on the kitchen table. The house downstairs was neat. The bed was made and undisturbed. However, he found the attic as represented in the model.

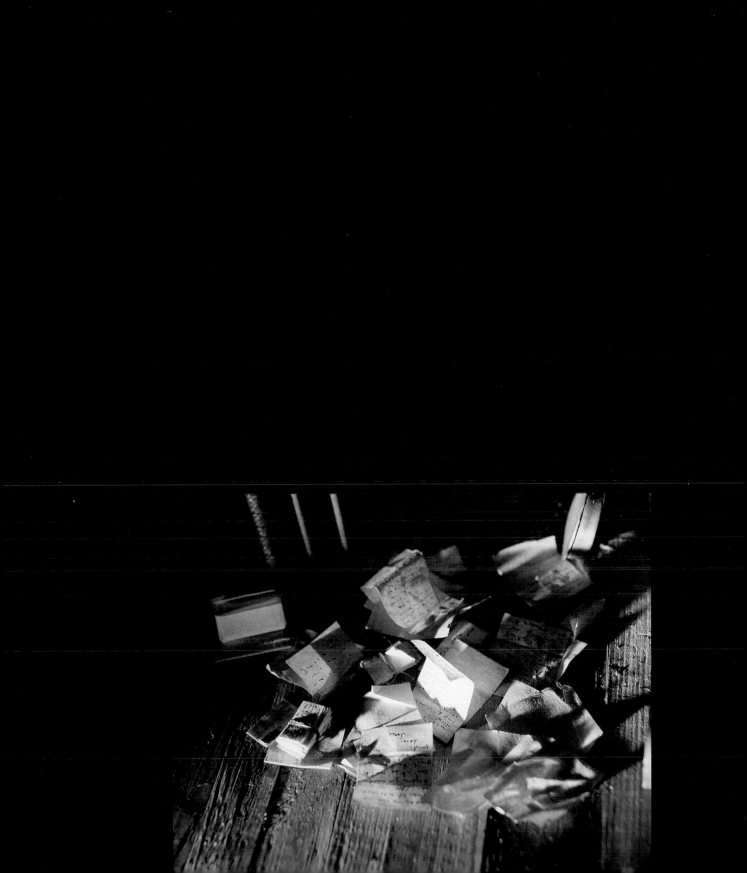

"The old are still accorded human rights. The dead, however, lose all rights from the very second of death. No law protects them any longer from slander, their privacy has ceased to be private; not even the letters written to them by their loved ones, not even the family album left to them by their mothers, nothing, nothing belongs to them any longer."

—Milan Kundera, *Immortality*

LAUNDRY LINE. When it was raining outside, people used to hang their laundry in the attic to dry. It's surprising that the line, made to hold laundry and not the weight of a person, didn't break or snap.

2 SPINNING WHEEL. "After the miller had boasted that his daughter could spin straw into gold, the king led the girl into a room filled with straw and said, 'If you don't spin this straw into gold by tomorrow morning, you must die.'"

—Rumplestiltskin in *Spells and Enchantment: The Wondrous Fairy Tales of Western Culture*

WARMING PAN. Before modern heat sources, hot coals were placed in a brass or copper container with a the long wooden handle, and the pan was moved between the sheets to produce warmth.

4 SHOE. One of Ms. Comptom's shoes is lying on the attic step. It is possible this shoe came off as Ms. Comptom was being hanged (either by suicide or homicide), or it may have come off as she struggled with a perpetrator who was dragging her into the attic. The backs of the shoes should be examined for abrasive damage consistent with being dragged.

5 OLD LETTERS. Old letters, taken out of the Governor Winthrop secretary desk, are scattered about the floor. They were presumably written by a former lover. Perhaps Jessie Comptom was depressed because she was growing old. The investigators would interview her friends and family and ask them if Jessie Comptom was despondent, if she was fixated on the past, or if she was leading an active life and making plans for the future. On the other hand, the letters could have been thrown on the floor as a suspect was searching the attic. The letters would be collected as evidence and processed for latent fingerprints.

6 CHAIR. The overturned chair may contain footwear impressions indicating Jessie Comptom stood on it prior to taking her life. The chair may also contain a suspect's shoe impressions as he hanged Jessie Comptom over the attic rafters.

7 CLOTHING. Jessie Comptom is very grandmotherly, with a flower print dress and apron, a shawl, and gray hair pulled back into a bun. She is found in the attic surrounded by numerous antiquated objects such as a phonograph, a quilt, and a warming pan. Moreover, the letters on the floor indicate that she may have committed suicide because she was growing old and nostalgic for the past.

8 KNOT. The investigators would cut the rope while preserving the knot. The knot may indicate if the person who tied it was left- or right-handed, or provide investigators with a clue about the occupation or hobby of the suspect. For example, is the knot one used by boaters? The investigators would look for drag or scuff marks on the rafters from hoisting the body up (in the case of a homicide). There may also be associated fraying of the rope. If the perpetrator killed the victim first, he might tie the rope around the neck and hoist the body up, rather than trying to maneuver the decedent's neck into the rope.

9 JESSIE COMPTOM. Ms. Comptom has what appear to be scratches and bruises on her face. This indicates that someone might have been trying to harm her. At autopsy, the full extent of Jessie Comptom's injuries would be documented.

Woodman's Shack

WILBY JENKS
dead

she lived with
HOMER CREGG & CARL STEBBIENS

REPORTED
THURSDAY, FEBRUARY 8, 1945

On Tuesday, February 6, 1945, at about 5:00 P.M., High Field Village Chief of Police

Lawrence W. Farmer was notified by Dr. George Barbour of High Field Village that there was a dead woman in a lumberman's camp on Pine Grove Road. Medical investigator Chester W. Dombay, Deputy Sheriff Thomas Gorman, photographer Adam Stanhope, and Chief Farmer went over at once. The deceased lived in a woodman's shack with Homer Cregg and Carl Stebbiens. Mr. Cregg and Mr. Stebbiens were both there very drunk. The body of Wilby Jenks was on the bed entirely covered with blankets, including her head and face. Chief Farmer pulled the blanket down and Stanhope took a picture. Dr. Dombay made an examination of the body and ordered it removed to a coffin in Graves Funeral Parlor. Mr. Stebbiens then laid down on the bed and photographer Stanhope took a picture of him, and also one of the outside of the shack. At the funeral parlor, Dr. Dombay again examined the body and found no marks of violence. Adam Stanhope then took another picture here. The two men were questioned that night and again the next day. Copies of Chief Farmer's and Dr. Dombay's reports are available.

The model shows the premise found by Dr. Barbour upon his arrival at 4:25 P.M., on Tuesday, February 6. Mr. Stebbiens is lying on the bed, also Wilby. Mr. Cregg is seated on the chair. News weather bureau reported weather clear, temperature 17°F. Sunset 5:03 P.M. Pacific Standard Time.

LOGGING TOOLS. Lee's carpenter, Ralph Mosher, made the logging tools. He also worked in the woods so he knew exactly what type of tools would be found in a woodman's shack. Hanging on the wall is a two-man crosscut saw with bow saw teeth (used to saw through large logs) and a peavey (used for lifting and maneuvering logs).

2 SHACK. Old pieces of wood were collected to make the model. The knots were of a specified size and placement. The wood was stained to make it appear consistent in color.

TRASH. The room paints a vivid picture of the inhabitants' impoverished lifestyle: three people lived in the crowded room, dirty dishes are on the table, bottles of liquor can be detected throughout, and the floor is littered with garbage and other objects.

4 BROKEN CHAIR. The chair back is broken. While this is in keeping with the ramshackle appearance of the room, the investigators would want to find out if the damage is new or old. It could have been broken during a dispute.

5 BEDDING. There is an incredible number of blankets on the bed. If Wilby Jenks pulled the covers over her head because she was cold, she could have suffocated—especially if she was intoxicated.

6 HOMER CREGG. Homer Cregg called Dr. George Barbour because he had a terrible pain in his side. The doctor examined him and wrote a prescription. As he was about to leave, one of the men asked him to look at a woman on the bed. The doctor examined the woman and found that she was dead and had perhaps been dead about two hours before he arrived. He had not noticed her until she was called to his attention. Upon returning to town, Dr. Barbour reported the matter to Chief Farmer.

7 WILBY JENKS. According to the report by the chief of police and the deputy sheriff, Wilby Jenks "had been at the camp a few weeks. We learned that plenty of drinking had been going on over the weekend. There were many beer and whiskey bottles there—of course all empty. Stebbiens appeared sort of dazed by the events. Cregg answered some questions and appeared very grieved over the death."

ANALYSES

The observations at the scene are not sufficient to determine cause and manner of death. There is limited information as well.

I would like to know if the three people had been in the shack all day, or did the men come home from work and find the victim deceased? The temperature outside was 17 degrees, but I would need to know the temperature inside. If the stove was not working, it would get cold very quickly inside, even if the victim was clothed and had blankets over her. Therefore, the cause could be hypothermia with the manner as accident. Even if all three were home all day together and it was cold inside, the woman would probably be more susceptible to the cold if she was smaller than the men. Liquor consumption would also cause the body to lose heat more rapidly. Whether or not the stove was functioning and whether the exhaust was blocked would also be a concern for carbon monoxide intoxication. The shack is dirty, with trash and liquor bottles strewn about, which may be attributed to sloppy housekeeping, often seen with substance abusers. This could also indicate some sort of domestic dispute. The age and past medical and social history of the victim is not revealed, which may be of interest in this case.

CHARLOTTE R. NORANBROCK, D-ABMDI, LEAD FORENSIC INVESTIGATOR

Barn

EBEN WALLACE
farmer, dead

MRS. EBEN WALLACE
wife, questioned

REPORTED
SATURDAY, JULY 15, 1939

MRS. WALLACE'S STATEMENT

Eben was hard to get along with. When he was irritated, he would go out to the barn, stand up on a bucket, put a noose around his neck, and threaten suicide.

I always talked him out of it. This afternoon, July 14, about four o'clock, we had an argument and he made the usual threats but I didn't follow him to the barn right away. When I did I found him hanging there with his feet through a wooden crate.

The bucket usually stood in the corner just inside the barn door, but yesterday I used it and left it out by the pump. The rope was always kept fastened to the beam just the way it was found—it was part of the regular barn hoist.

The model shows the premises as Mrs. Wallace found them.

1 **BARN.** Barn was the first model Lee made. It took three months to build and was assembled from strips of weathered wood, timbers, and old planks that were removed from a one-hundred-year-old barn.[9] They were run through a table saw and thereby cut to scale. The floorboards leading to the barn were worn down where the machinery came in and out. An article in the *Boston Herald* notes that an actual spiderweb in the haymow had to be removed because it was "12 times too big."

2 **HORSESHOE.** Horseshoes are seen as a token of good luck and a protection against evil spirits. They are commonly hung above the doorways of barns, stables, and dwellings.

3 **TRACTOR MARKS.** Some detectives-in-training hypothesize that the tractor marks were freshly made by a truck that hoisted Eben Wallace into his hanged position.

4 **HAY HOIST.** "In order not to identify the case I changed the locale to a barn and used the fall from the hay hoist in which to make the noose. Since this hay hoist was not in all probability kept in its present position means employed for placing the sled in the loft) I am inclined to think that its undisturbed position is questionable. Moreover, here in New England in a farm family such as would own this barn the woman of the family attends to the house, the man takes charge of the barn and neither one is likely to know the details of how things are kept in the domain cared for by the other."[10]

5 **PICTURESQUE LANDSCAPE.** "The country comes to stand not only for nature but also for permanence in a world where so much else is threatened by undesirable change. As a result, the potentially political material of the modern city was largely eschewed and the setting of the country house and picturesque village became the norm, with the attendant predictable irony of the surprise of crime. W. H. Auden defined such a setting as 'the Great Good Place,' adding, 'the more Eden like it is, the greater the contradiction of murder.'"
—Dennis Porter, *The Pursuit of Crime: Art and Ideology in Detective Fiction*

6 **OX YOKE.** Lee painted the ox yoke with old-fashioned blue wagon paint and then dragged it by a string along a dusty road to make it look old

7 **HANGED FARMER.** "If you got your eyes down to the level of the doorway you soon forgot you were looking at a model, and your eye wandered in and out to see what all the farmer had in store there. It was something of a shock to see the farmer himself hanging by the neck from one of the upper timbers."
—John Lee, *Family Reunion*

8 **SUICIDE OR ACCIDENTAL DEATH?** If Eben Wallace's death were ruled a suicide his wife would collect the face value of his life insurance contract. If it were ruled accidental, she would be eligible for double indemnity, that is, if he died under accidental circumstances the beneficiary would collect twice the face amount of the policy.

9. William Gilman, "Murder at Harvard," *Boston Herald*, January 1948, 5.

10. Frances Glessner Lee, correspondence with Alan Moritz, M.D., The Harvard Medical Library in the Francis A. Countway Library of Medicine, Boston, 1945.

Saloon and Jail

FRANK HARRIS
dock laborer, dead

DENNIS MULCAHEY
city patrolman, questioned

REPORTED
SUNDAY, NOVEMBER 12, 1944

DENNIS MULCAHEY'S STATEMENT

On Saturday night, November 11th at 11:30 P.M., I was walking my beat on Dock Street.

I saw a man lying sprawled out on the sidewalk in front of Pat's Place, a saloon. The man was breathing and smelt strongly of liquor. I called the wagon which took the man to Station Two, where he was locked up in a single cell. His Union card bore the name of Frank Harris, address Twenty-seven and a half Walter Street. He appeared to be very drunk. There were no marks of violence on him. On Sunday morning, November 12th at 7:00 when rounds were made in Station Two, Mr. Harris was found dead in his cell, as represented by the model.

SALOON AND JAIL

1 **CANDY/CIGARS VERSUS ALE/BEER.** Oscar G. Rejlander's famous allegorical photograph of 1857, *The Two Ways of Life*, depicts two young men guided by a sage on their way to manhood. One looks toward the left side of the image, which shows a life of gambling, drinking, and other vices, while the other man looks toward the right, which depicts piety and industry. This model also presents two possible paths. On the left side of the scene the

window of the Candy and Cigar shop displays wholesome American items such as baseball bats and gloves, a pair of roller skates, lollypops, peanuts, a harmonica, a stack of comics, and various magazines—one with a picture of the Statue of Liberty, another entitled *American Home*, one with a headline that reads "Air Power," and a copy of *Newsweek* with a cover story about the upcoming election. The window of Pat's Pub displays less wholesome American

traditions—pin-up girls and bottles of liquor. Young Mr. Harris is depicted in front of the latter.

2 **PAT'S PLACE.** The investigators would ask the bar owner: Who was drinking? Was Frank Harris drinking? How long was he there? Did he have an altercation? How much did he drink?

3 **HARVARD HAS WHAT IT TAKES.** The sign in the window

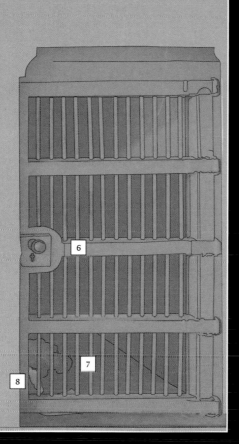

of Pat's Place reads HARVARD HAS
WHAT IT TAKES. The bar is presumably
a Boston pub and might have been in
the vicinity of Harvard, or the sign may
have been hung to show allegiance with
a Harvard sports team. It was also a way
to advertise Harvard University, where
the models were displayed.

4 **DOCK STREET.** The majority
of the models re-created New
England settings. The sign HARVARD
HAS WHAT IT TAKES situates *Saloon
and Jail* in Boston. Details that tip us
off in other scenes include: the New
Hampshire license plates in *Garage*,
local newspapers, the postcard of
the Old Man of the Mountain in *Blue*

Bedroom, and vernacular architecture
such as the log cabin and barn.

5 **BANANA PEEL.** He could have
slipped on the banana peel!

6 **JAIL.** The medical examiner
performs an autopsy anytime
someone dies in police custody.

7 **HAT/HEAD INJURY.** Blane
Vucci, Baltimore city detective,
points out that if Frank Harris had a
head injury under his hat and lost blood
in the jail cell, he would have symptoms
like he was drunk when in fact he
was really comatose. Often with head
injuries or overdose, the fluid drains

through the nasal cavities, ear, etc.
Investigators would search the jail cell
as well as the interior of his cap for the
presence of blood.

8 **FRANK HARRIS.** At autopsy, the
medical examiner would collect
tissue, blood, and other body fluids.
These fluids, particularly the blood,
would be submitted to the forensic toxicologist, and blood alcohol levels would
be determined. Any other controlled
dangerous substances Mr. Harris
had ingested would be identified. At
autopsy, the medical examiner would
attempt to discern any other trauma or
disease that would have contributed to
Frank Harris's death.

Striped Bedroom

RICHARD HARVEY
foreman in an ice-cream factory, dead

MRS. MARY HARVEY
mother, questioned

REPORTED
Monday, April 29, 1940

MARY HARVEY'S STATEMENT

On Saturday night, April 27th, Richard came home for supper and after supper he went back to work.

He always worked late Saturday nights to get ready for the Sunday trade. I don't know when he came home because I went to bed early. Sunday morning I let him sleep while I went to church and then, as usual, went to my sister's for the day. When I returned home Sunday evening, Richard wasn't around so I opened his door and found him dead in his bed.

Richard was married about a year ago and brought his wife home to live. She was a nice girl and they were very happy. His wife is away now visiting her parents for a few days in another state. Richard was a good boy but sometimes he had a little too much to drink, especially on Saturday nights. The dishpan belonged in the kitchen. I don't know why it's in Richard's bedroom.

Mary Harvey found the premises as represented by the model.

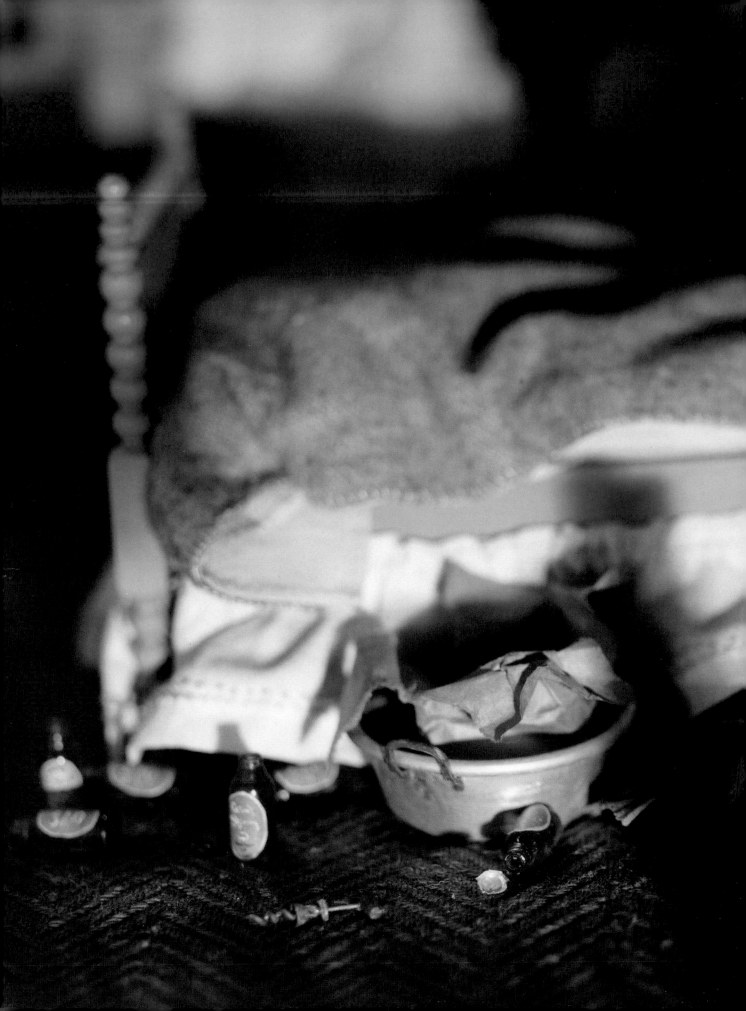

Striped Bedroom

1 **BOX**. What is inside the unopened box?

2 **CLOTHES ON CHAIR**. The outfit that Richard Harvey wore, a blue shirt and black pants, are laid out on the chair. This informs the investigators of his actions: he undressed and got ready for bed.

3 **FLOWERED WALLPAPER**. Striped Bedroom is extremely feminine: flowered wallpaper, flowered chair and ottoman, delicate ruffle curtains, and a flowered pattern on the furniture. One gets the impression that Richard Harvey not only lived under his mother's roof, but also under her thumb. Was he overwhelmed by the women in his life? How did his wife feel about living with her mother-in-law?

4 **THE OBJECTS OF A DEAD MAN**. "There is nothing more terrible, I learned, than having to face the objects of a dead man. Things are inert: they have meaning only in function of the life that makes use of them. When that life ends, the things change, even though they remain the same. They are there and yet not there: tangible ghosts, condemned to survive in a world they no longer belong to. What is one to think, for example, of a closetful of clothes waiting silently to be worn again by a man who will not be coming back to open the door? Or the stray packets of condoms strewn among brimming drawers of underwear and

socks? Or an electric razor sitting in the bathroom, still clogged with the whisker dust of the last shave? Or a dozen empty tubes of hair coloring hidden away in a leather traveling case?—suddenly revealing things one has no desire to see, no desire to know. There is a poignancy to it, and also a kind of horror. In themselves, the things mean nothing, like the cooking utensils of some vanished civilization. And yet they say something to us, standing there not as objects but as remnants of thought, of consciousness, emblems of the solitude in which a man comes to make decisions about himself: whether to color his hair, whether to wear this or that shirt, whether to live, whether to die. And the futility of it all once there is death."
—Paul Auster, *The Invention of Solitude*

5 **BIBLE**. Did Richard Harvey read the Bible every night before going to sleep, or every morning after waking up?

6 **BED**. Seven corpses in the Nutshell Studies are depicted in their beds. The bed is loaded with meaning. It is the most private place in the house. It is where one dreams, retreats in ill health, performs sex, and conceives a child. People are most vulnerable when sleeping—they are in a place that is supposed to be "safe." Sadly, many of the corpses appear as if they are peacefully sleeping.

7 **BOTTLES OF LIQUOR**. Some of the liquor bottles appear full. The investigators would perform a blood alcohol level test to find out whether Richard Harvey was intoxicated.

8 **BASIN**. The basin was filled with dry ice, which suggests that Richard Harvey wanted to chill his beer.

9 **RICHARD HARVEY.** Richard Harvey's core temperature, as well as the degree of rigor and livor mortis development, will provide investigators with an estimate of when death occurred.

Living Room

MRS. RUBY DAVIS
housewife, dead

REGINALD DAVIS
husband, questioned

REPORTED
FRIDAY, MAY 22, 1941

REGINALD DAVIS'S STATEMENT

My wife and I spent last night [Thursday, May 21]
quietly at home. She went upstairs to bed
shortly before I did.

This morning I woke up a little before 5:00 to find my wife was no longer
beside me. After waiting a while, I got up to see where she was and found
her dead on the stairs. I called our doctor right away and when he got here
he immediately notified the police.

The model shows the premises just before the arrival of the family physician.

Living Room

1 **RADIO**. The Philco Radio was from a line of custom-built dollhouse furniture by Strombecker, a company known for producing accurately scaled furniture.[11]

2 **PHONE**. Why did Reginald Davis call the doctor, instead of the police, after finding his wife dead?

3 **TEN CIGARETTES**. Does Reginald Davis smoke *Lucky Strikes*? Are all butts of the same brand? These butts should be collected as evidence.

4 **LIGHTING**. The empty armchair and corpse are the two illuminated aspects in this scene. Lee carefully lit each

model. She considered the intensity of the light and how it defined the interior space, using twelve- and fourteen-volt bulbs (some were flashlight bulbs). When installed at Harvard, the models were recessed into the walls of a totally black room, thus accentuating their moody atmospheres. The text accompanying each case was hung above the models with a shaded light that gave "just enough illumination to permit the students to walk safely in the room… but would not detract from the light in the models themselves," according to Lee. [12]

5 **COMFORTABLE CHAIR**. Anthony Vidler quotes Ernst Bloch, in *The Architectural Uncanny:*

Essays in the Modern Unhomely, "The setting in which detective stories are enjoyed the most is just too cozy. In a comfortable chair, under the nocturnal floor lamp with tea, rum, and tobacco, personally secure and peacefully immersed in dangerous things."[13] *Living Room* has all the accouterments that Bloch describes: a comfortable chair, floor lamp, tobacco, and detective story.

6 **NEWSPAPERS**. Books and newspapers are tossed about on the floor, including the *Littleton Courier* (the newspaper in the town where Lee lived), *Newsweek*, and the *Boston Herald*. One headline reads, "Huge Yank Forces Bomb Reich." Lee solicited numerous

newspapers for front pages with large, clearly printed headlines. The front page was photographically reduced to two-by-three-inch plates and a 1/2-inch newspaper was printed from the plates. The tiny newspaper was then sewn together and the edges were torn to reproduce a newspaper's jagged edge.[14]

7 THE SIGN OF THE FOUR.

"You see," he said with a significant raising of the eyebrows. In the light of the lantern I read with a thrill of horror, "The sign of the four."

"In god's name, what does it mean?" I asked.

"It means murder," said he, stooping over the dead man. "Ah! I expected it. Look here."

He pointed to what looked like a long dark thorn stuck in the skin just above the ear.

"It looks like a thorn," said I.

"It is a thorn. You may pick it out. But be careful, for it is poisoned."
—Sir Arthur Conan Doyle, *The Sign of the Four*

8 PAINTING OF A HOUSE.

Hanging above the hearth is a painting of a peaceful house surrounded by lush green foliage. The house sits beside a dirt road lined with birch trees that leads to a distant clearing. The happy and secure house in the painting counterbalances the destroyed home. The painting is reminiscent of a photograph that hung above the Glessners' fireplace in Chicago of Abingdon Abbey, a rural, preindustrial building that served as the prototype for H. H. Richardson's design of Glessner House. In reality, the painting is a representation of Lee's cottage on the Rocks estate. Lee made her house the symbol of the unattained ideal to which the family in *Living*

Room aspired. Her carpenter surmised that she incorporated a miniature painting of her own house in a Nutshell Study "because she was so proud of it."[15]

9 HEAD. Clue: the head of the body.

10 RUBY DAVIS. At autopsy, medical examiners would determine if Mrs. Davis's injuries were consistent with a fall.

11. Dian Zillner, *American Dollhouses and Furniture from the 20th Century* (Atglen, Penn.: Schiffer Publishing, 1995), 45.
12. Correspondence between Lee and Alan Moritz, April 21, 1945, Francis A. Countway Library of Medicine.
13. Anthony Vidler, *The Architectural Uncanny: Essays in the Modern Unhomely* (Cambridge, Mass.: MIT Press, 1992), 4.
14. Richard F. Dempewolff, "Mysterious Death Their Business," *Popular Mechanics* 100, no. 1 (July 1953): 240.
15. Alton Mosher, interview with Corinne Botz, Salem, N.H., June 2002.

Two-Story Porch

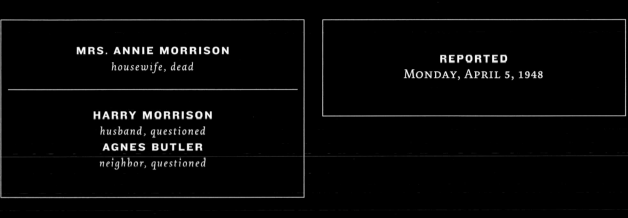

MRS. ANNIE MORRISON
housewife, dead

HARRY MORRISON
husband, questioned
AGNES BUTLER
neighbor, questioned

REPORTED
MONDAY, APRIL 5, 1948

HARRY MORRISON'S STATEMENT

I have a job on the late shift but was up earlier than usual today, April 5th, because I didn't work

yesterday, which was Sunday. At about 11:00 I was in the kitchen on the top story where my wife and I live. My wife did the weeks wash and was standing on a chair hanging it out to dry. I heard a sort of noise and went to see what it was, and found her lying on the ground below.

AGNES BUTLER'S STATEMENT

I live in the apartment below the Morrisons.

I bathed the baby this morning, and put him in his carriage. I had his weeks wash and hung it out to dry. I was cleaning up the kitchen when I heard a crash and rushed onto the porch and saw Annie lying on the ground below. The Morrisons quarreled a lot and Harry didn't treat his wife very well. He drank sometimes and Annie guessed he had lady friends. I heard them arguing this morning.

TWO-STORY PORCH. The model shows the back side of a two-story duplex. The building probably replicated a duplex in a working class Boston neighborhood or nearby suburb. The Butlers' porch, which is equipped with a swing, icebox, and sunblind, is an extension of their house and serves as a combination living and service area. Mrs. Butler can keep an eye on the baby while she performs household chores. The Morrisons' porch, on the other hand, does not have any furniture and appears to serve a solely utilitarian purpose.

CHAIR. Investigators should search the interior of the apartment and balcony for any evidence that may help determine why Annie Morrison fell off the balcony. Was the chair leg loose or broken? Is there a greasy residue on the chair seat?

3 ICE CARD. The ice card is hung on the porch window so that it's visible to the iceman as he makes his rounds. Each ice card has a number that represents various pounds of ice. The number at the top of the card designates how much ice should be delivered on the said day. On Monday, April 5, the Butlers requested ten pounds of ice.

4 AGNES BUTLER. Dr. Alan R. Moritz, who served as head of the Harvard Department of Legal Medicine, investigated a case on which Lee might have based *Two-Story Porch*. In a 1941 article, the *Boston Sunday Post* described the case:

That morning the husband and wife who lived in a duplex house in a nearby suburb had words. Loud and clarion words, to hear the neighbors tell it. The wife's words were particularly shrill. She was a woman who was likely to fly into a rage at the drop of her husband's least peccadillo.

Following the embroglio, the husband left the house and all was still, too still to please the neighbor in the other half of the duplex house. She was a somewhat curious lady. Hearing no sound whatever through the not-at-all-sound-proof partition, the neighbor investigated and found the wife lying dead on the bathroom floor.[16]

While the neighbor (like Mrs. Butler) was pretty certain the husband killed the wife, Dr. Moritz's autopsy found that the cause of her death was apoplexy, which was brought on by her fit of rage at her husband.

5 CLOTHING. Annie Morrison is wearing typical housewife attire of the period: a hairnet, a brown dress covered with a gingham popover dress (a popular dress style designed by Claire McCardell in 1942), an apron with a shamrock print, a knit sweater vest, and stockings. Like all the dolls, she wears underwear: in this instance, white bloomers.

6 ANNIE MORRISON. A crime lab employee should measure the distance Mrs. Morrison is lying from the apartment building. This measurement may support a jump, push, or fall hypothesis.

The nature of Annie Morrison's injuries and the cause of her death will likely be revealed during autopsy. If Mrs. Morrison suffered a stroke or a heart attack, for example, investigators can conclude that her death was accidental. Blood alcohol levels and the presence of controlled dangerous substances should be checked, as they may have contributed to her death.

According to Jerry Dziecichowicz, Chief Administrator of Baltimore Medical Examiner's Office, investigators who were assigned *Two-Story Dwelling* responded with "boos and hisses" because it is difficult—if not impossible—to solve. It is therefore no longer assigned to detectives-in-training. *Two-Story Porch* is a testament to Dr. George Burgess Magrath's maxim: "Death occurs in queer places and under strange circumstances. Sometimes we just miss keeping alive."[17]

ANALYSES
The observations at the scene are consistent with a fall:
1. The laundry was neatly hung, not disturbed.
2. The chair is leaning on the railing.
3. The railing has pulled away from the post on one side next to the chair. This is consistent with the weight of a body falling against the railing.
4. One towel is on the railing and one is on the ground (held and/or over the shoulder).
5. The decedent's clothing appears to be intact, along with the hairnet.
6. A flower box on the first level was partially pulled off the railing. Had there been some sort of struggle prior to her fall, it is likely the laundry and her clothing would have been disturbed/disheveled. However, an autopsy is still necessary to rule out foul play. (Did the decedent have a prior head injury due to a domestic assault which would cause her to collapse?) Also, the possibility still exists that her husband could have quietly come out to the porch and pushed her over. Therefore, a skilled interrogator should be assigned to question the husband.

**CHARLOTTE R. NORANBROCK, D-ABMDI,
LEAD FORENSIC INVESTIGATOR**

16. Charles P. Haven, "Colleges Join Police In Hunting Down Killers," *Boston Sunday Post*, November 30, 1941, A-5.

17. "Dr. Magrath Dies Suddenly," *Boston Globe*, December 12, 1938, 4.

Kitchen

ROBIN BARNES
housewife, dead

FRED BARNES
husband, questioned

REPORTED
WEDNESDAY, APRIL 12, 1944

FRED BARNES'S STATEMENT

About 4:00 on the afternoon of Tuesday, April 11th, I went downtown on an errand for my wife.

I returned about an hour and a half later and found the outside door to the kitchen locked. It was propped open when I left. I knocked and called but got no answer. I then tried the front door but it was also locked. I went to the kitchen window which was closed and locked. I looked in and saw what appeared to be my wife lying on the floor. I sent for the police.

The model shows the premises just before the police forced open the kitchen door.

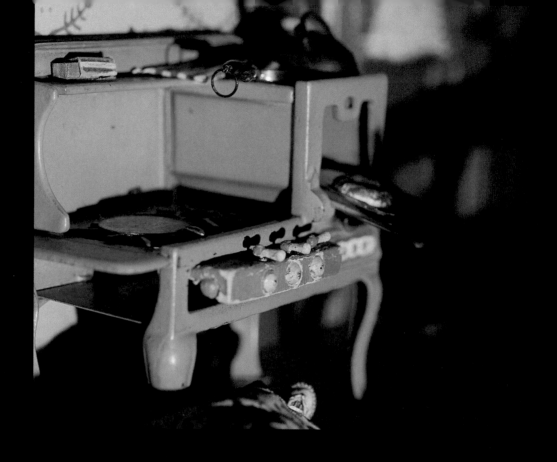

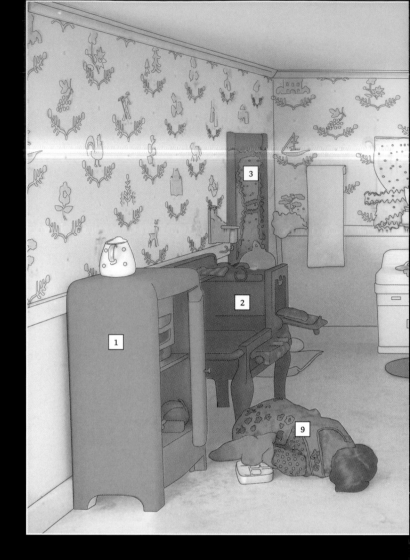

KITCHEN

1 DOLL KITCHEN. A tradition of doll kitchens began in Germany during the early nineteenth century. The doll kitchen was taken out each year for the Christmas season and supplied with a few items from the real kitchen. Through doll kitchens, young girls familiarized themselves with the kitchen and practiced for their intended role in the home. The kitchens were based on human-sized kitchens and developed according to innovations in

the household.[18] Similarly, the model *Kitchen* is a realistic portrayal of a certain type of American kitchen from the mid-1940s.

2 GAS JETS. The gas jets on the stove are open.

3 DOORS. If both doors are locked from the inside, how could a murderer have escaped?

4 HALF-PEELED POTATOES. Robin Barnes was involved in a number of domestic tasks in various stages of completion. Investigators studying this scene commonly interpret this in either of the following ways: (1) There are many activities but only one finished task —the cake. Mrs. Barnes appears to have been upset, preoccupied and unable to concentrate. She finally decided to commit suicide, which she had been probably contemplating for a

long time. (2) This is a realistic portrayal of a woman performing multiple household chores. It is suspicious that Robin Barnes decided to commit suicide in the middle of making dinner—suicide is not an impulsive decision. Furthermore, why would she cook dinner if she was on the brink of suicide?

5 **TABLE.** The table and tablecloth are askew in an otherwise harmonious kitchen.

6 **KNIFE.** The knife on the chair was presumably used to stuff the newspaper in the cracks around the doorframe, thereby sealing off the room so no carbon monoxide could escape.

7 **BEVERAGE.** There is a drink on the table and it looks like someone was sitting there. Did Robin Barnes have company? The can would be collected as evidence. Once at the Crime Lab, the can would be swabbed for possible DNA evidence and subsequently processed for latent fingerprints. The ice trays on the floor adjacent to Mrs. Barnes's body suggest she may have been getting ice for a visitor's drink.

8 **VANITAS.** There are many still lifes in the models, and they are reminiscent of vanitas, a type of seventeenth-century Dutch still-life painting, which represents the vanity of life and encroachment of death

through objects such as skulls, burning candles, and musical instruments. Unlike traditional vanitas, in the Nutshells, death has arrived and repentance is futile.

9 **CORPSE.** The rosy hue of the corpse indicates carbon monoxide poisoning.

18. Eva Stille and Severin Stille, *Doll Kitchens: 1800–1980*, (West Chester, Penn.: Schiffer Publishing, 1988).

Garage

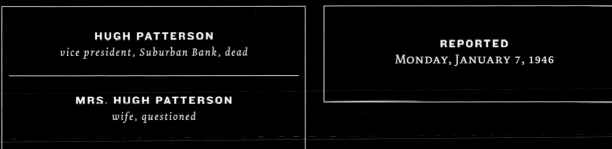

HUGH PATTERSON
vice president, Suburban Bank, dead

MRS. HUGH PATTERSON
wife, questioned

REPORTED
Monday, January 7, 1946

MRS. PATTERSON'S STATEMENT

Hugh went out alone in the car after dinner on Saturday, January 5th. He often did this,

especially lately, and would stay out very late. Sunday morning he hadn't come home at breakfast time so I went to the garage to see if the car was there. I looked in the left-hand door and saw him hanging out of the car. I telephoned the police station for help because I couldn't reach the doctor. Hugh seemed troubled for a while now and money wasn't as plentiful as it once was. Some time ago he told me that he carried heavy life insurance, with the double indemnity clause for accident, in my favor. About that time he deeded the house over to me. He had begun to drink a good deal lately.

The patrolman, upon arrival, went around to the back, broke the glass, climbed in the window and opened both doors. He left, again through the window so as not to disturb footprints in front. He found the garage full of gas, the car's ignition turned on, the tank empty.

The model shows the premises just after the patrolman left the garage by way of the window.

Garage

1 **FOOTPRINTS**. "The footprints are suspicious," notes Abby Glenn, an investigator with Maryland Medical Examiner's Office. "The wife's story about going and looking into the left door are accounted for; however, there is a second pair of footprints leading away from the scene that are not. In this particular case I would also want to know if the heater in the car was on, if there are tire tracks in the snow, if the garage floor is wet—

supporting the idea that he did go on his usual drive."

2 **GARAGE DOORS**. The garage doors were handmade by Lee's carpenter. They were inlaid with glass and each one has hinges, making it possible to fold and unfold them. When closed, there is a piece of pipe on the bottom of the door that can be turned to go into the cement and secure the door in place.

3 **WALLS**. The walls in *Garage* were made by cutting bricks to size and laying each one out with mortar.

4 **SPARE TIRE**. Lee bought two of the same manufactured cars. She removed the tire and hung it on the wall as a spare. The car was repainted red.

5 **POSTER**. TIME TO RE-TIRE. GET A FISK was a famous poster for Fisk Tire Co. The poster, hanging near

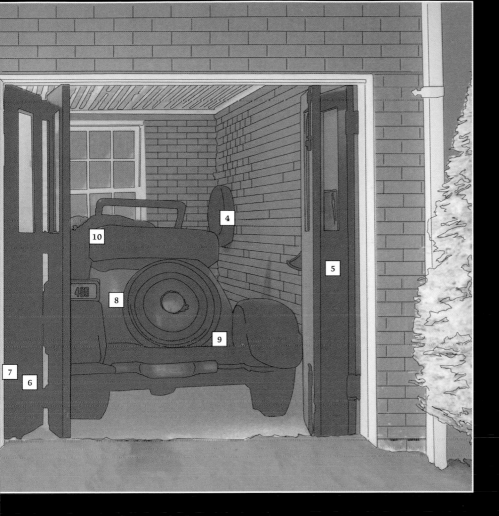

the "retired" body of Hugh Patterson, becomes black humor.

6 **HAT.** Lee made the hat by steaming old felt and placing it into a mold, shaping it, then putting a band around it. She would often reenact events with her carpenter, having him fall in certain ways to get the proper position for a hat.

7 **POKER.** The poker is lying on the floor in a haphazard manner, which is not in keeping with the relatively tidy garage. Investigators would collect the fire poker as possible evidence. Pending autopsy findings, the poker may need to be examined for

the presence of blood and processed for latent fingerprints.

8 **VEHICLE.** Investigators would search the garage and the interior of the vehicle thoroughly for evidence that Hugh Patterson committed suicide. Items that support this determination include a good-bye note, personal keepsakes, or photographs located in close proximity to Hugh Patterson.

9 **GAS TANK.** The gas tank is empty and the garage doors and window were closed. This might be a case of suicide through carbon monoxide poisoning.

10 **HUGH PATTERSON.** At autopsy, the medical examiner would collect samples of tissue, blood, and other body fluids. These samples would be sent to a forensic toxicologist to determine, among other things, blood alcohol and carbon monoxide levels. Investigators at the crime scene may be able to make a preliminary determination about the cause of death based upon the color of Hugh Patterson's skin. Lethal levels of carbon monoxide turn an individual's skin a characteristic cherry red color. This is particularly true in areas where lividity (postmortem settling of the blood) has developed.

Parsonage Parlor

DOROTHY DENNISON
high school student, dead

MRS. JAMES DENNISON
questioned by police lieutenant Robert Peal

REPORTED
Friday, August 23, 1946

MRS. DENNISON'S STATEMENT

On Monday, August 19th, Dorothy walked to town to buy some hamburger steak for dinner. She didn't have much money in her purse.

When she failed to return in time for dinner I telephoned a neighbor who told me she saw Dorothy walking toward the market, but had not seen her since. I also telephoned the market and the owner said he sold Dorothy a pound of hamburger sometime before noon but didn't notice which way she turned when she left his shop. By late afternoon, thoroughly alarmed, I notified the police.

Lieutenant Peal's investigation report stated that Monday afternoon, August 19, 1946, at 5:25 P.M., he received a telephone call from Mrs. Dennison at police headquarters, and at once took charge of the matter personally. The customary inquiries began by Wednesday. A systematic search of all closed or unoccupied buildings in the vicinity was undertaken. It was not until Friday, August 23, at 4:15, he and Officer Patrick Sullivan entered the Parsonage Parlor and found the premises as represented in the model.

Temperatures during the week ranged from between 86 and 92°F with high humidity.

1 **SYMMETRY/PAIRS.** The room is remarkably symmetrical and paired: two vases on the piano, two painting of flowers in vases on either side of the piano, two windows, two sofas beneath the window, two light fixtures, two religious images hanging beneath the light fixtures, two wooden chairs on either side of the room. The corpse disrupts the order and balance. The missing pair for the corpse can either be interpreted as the perpetrator or the girl's mother.

2 **PIANO.** There may be blood on the piano and keys. Investigators should question Mrs. Dennison to determine if her daughter could play the piano. It is possible that Dorothy Dennison was invited into the parlor and asked to play a song, and was initially attacked from behind, possibly with the hammer. Consequently, the piano keys should also be processed for latent fingerprints.

3 **COVERED FURNITURE.** The rector of the church, who resides in this house, has apparently gone on vacation for the summer months. Two ghostlike armchairs are covered with fabric, the freestanding lights are covered and tied with fabric, the rug is rolled up, the curtains have been removed from the rods, the windows are shut and the window blinds are down and closed. Beneath the mail slot, a small pile of letters has accumulated.

4 **MADONNA AND CHILD.** In her discussion of Madonna and Child paintings, Anne Higonnet notes that by the late eighteenth and nineteenth centuries, Madonna and Child painting were secularized and came to stand for a general maternity. Higonnet writes, "Depending on your point of view, identification of women with the image of a mother worshiping her child could be

either conservative or progressive, self-abasing or empowering, disembodying or erotic. In some ways, women denied their own bodies by identifying maternity with the Renaissance Madonna and Child image. Most obviously, they narrowed down female sexuality to maternity, which suited sexually conservative men perfectly well."[19]

5 **JOURNEY OF THE MAGI.** The calendar depicts the Magi following the star to Bethlehem to adorn baby Jesus with gifts. The celebration of life and giving in the image are a striking contrast to Dorothy's death and the wrapped package of hamburger meat (directly beneath the painting), which she was *traveling* home to give her mother.

6 **HAMBURGER MEAT.** The package of rancid hamburger meat versus the condition of Dorothy Dennison's body will assist investigators in estimating the time of death.

7 **CLOTHING.** There is a romanticized quality to the girl's outfit. She is wearing a white tunic-style dress, red lace-up ballet shoes, a red belt, and a red bow in her hair. Her matching red wallet is beside the meat. The victim is represented by the colors red and white, symbolic of innocence destroyed.

8 **BITE MARKS.** There are bite marks on the victim's torso and legs. Crime lab personnel today would swab the victim's skin in the vicinity of the bite marks for saliva, which may contain DNA. The bite impressions would be photographically documented and, once the corpse arrived at the medical examiner's office, the wounds would likely be excised and preserved for possible comparison. The medical examiner would also determine if these impressions were made premortem or

postmortem. If a suspect developed, a forensic odontologist would obtain casts and bite impressions of the suspect's teeth and determine whether the bite marks on the victim could have been made by the suspect. A DNA sample would also be collected from the suspect for comparison with that recovered from the swabs of the victim's skin.

9 **DOROTHY DENNISON.** The position of Ms. Dennison is suspicious. It appears that her body was displayed. Photographs of the body and overall crime scene would be sent to a forensic psychiatrist for evaluation.

ANALYSES
It is likely that she willingly went to this place as the meat and purse are placed on the chair, not thrown about or left somewhere else (i.e., where she might have initially been accosted). She probably knew the killer as she either went there with him or let him in (assuming no sign of forced entry) and there are no signs of a struggle at the crime scene. The killer was able to get close enough to stab her or hit her (with the hammer) without her apparently fighting or trying to escape (knocking things over, etc.). We would need to know what the autopsy said regarding the cause of death (hammer to head? stab to abdomen?) and whether or not a sexual assault took place, and if so, whether it was pre- or postmortem.

MICHAEL MCGRATH, M.D.
CONSULTANT IN FORENSIC PSYCHIATRY
AND CRIMINAL PROFILING

19. Anne Higonnet, *Pictures of Innocence: The History and Crisis of Ideal Childhood* (London: Thames and Hudson, 1998), 39–45.

Red Bedroom

MARIE JONES
prostitute, dead

MRS. SHIRLEY FLANAGAN
landlord, questioned
JIM GREEN
boyfriend and client of Marie's, questioned

REPORTED
THURSDAY, JUNE 29, 1944

This morning [Thursday, June 29] I passed the open door of Marie's room and called out "hello."

When no one answered I looked in and found Marie's body in the closet and immediately called the police.

Jim Green, a boyfriend and client of Marie's, came in with her yesterday afternoon. I don't know when he left. After telephoning the police, I found Mr. Green and brought him in for questioning.

I met Marie on the sidewalk yesterday afternoon

and we walked to a nearby store where I bought two bottles of whiskey. We went to her room and sat smoking and drinking for a while. Marie was sitting in the big chair; she got really drunk. All of a sudden she grabbed my open jacket knife, which I'd used to cut the string around the package containing the bottles. She ran into the closet and shut the door. When I opened the door I found her lying there. I immediately left the house.

The model shows the premises as Mr. Green found them.

1 BOTTLES OF WHISKEY. Why are the bottles knocked over? Today, the bottles of whiskey would be collected as evidence and returned to the Crime Lab where they would be swabbed for DNA and processed for latent fingerprints. These steps would be taken in investigators' attempts to substantiate Mr. Green's version of the events that transpired preceding Marie Jones's death.

2 BONBONS. Were the bonbons a gift? Did Jim Green buy them for Marie Jones after an argument? The bonbon box may contain latent fingerprints, and the candies inside could harbor fingerprints, bite marks, DNA, or poison. The box would be collected as evidence and, if necessary to the case, traced back to the store from which it was purchased.

3 WINDOW. In the models, the windows connect the inside and the outside, the living and the dead. Sometimes the scenes they reveal appear to offer hope or provide metaphorical glimpses of the afterlife. However, because the windows failed as an escape route for the victims, they are ultimately a point of vulnerability where the perpetrator may have entered or exited. Windows permit real and symbolic invasion.

4 RED BEDROOM. *Red Bedroom* takes its place alongside red rooms in film and literature. Agent Cooper's infamous dreams in *Twin Peaks* occur in a red room, which is also the name of a gothic thriller by H. G. Wells. One of the most famous red room scenes is in *Jane Eyre*. Jane is locked inside the terrifying red room, where her uncle Mr. Reed died, after an argument with her cousin. She suffers a fit:

My heart beat thick, my head grew hot; a sound filled my ears, which I deemed the rushing of wings: something seemed near me; I was oppressed, suffocated: endurance broke down—I uttered a wild, involuntary cry—I rushed to the door and shook the lock in desperate effort.

Jane never fully recovers from this breakdown. In *The Madwoman in the Attic*, Sandra M. Gilbert and Susan Gubar describe the room as a "patriarchal death chamber" and point out, "Jane's pilgrimage consists of a series of experiences which are, in one way or another, variations on the central, red-room motif of enclosure and escape."[20]

5 ROSE. Dante used the rose as a symbol of paradise. The rose also signifies beauty, love, war, and because it's ephemeral, death and the afterlife. Note: the only living entity in the scene is the red rose in the planter outside the window.

6 BED. The 1836 murder of Helen Jewett, a beautiful prostitute, provoked a national sensation. Jewett was killed in a New York City brothel by blows to her head with a hatchet. Afterward, in an effort to conceal his crime, the murderer set on fire the bed where the corpse lay. Despite substantial evidence linking Richard P. Robinson, Jewett's wealthy client and lover, to the murder, he was not convicted and the crime was never solved. According to Katherine Ramsland, "As with the trial, the attitude of the day was that men could be absolved of their sexual transgressions (including murder) because female sexuality inspired it."[21] Helen Jewett's murder inspired numerous fictionalized tales of the murder; it is often compared to the murder of Mary Rogers, which served as the basis for Edgar Allen Poe's *The Murder of Marie Roget*.

7 MOOSE PAINTING. According to Native American symbolism, the moose represents "scrutiny and attention to detail." As the largest member of the deer family that is known to charge dangerously without warning, it is also symbolic of masculinity and unpredictability.

8 SUITCASE. Is the suitcase filled with clothing?

9 MARIE JONES. "The dead lady in the closet of the red bedroom has gold bangles on both wrists and wears scarlet lipstick and dark red nail polish. She is quite tough."
—Frances Glessner Lee

"Females identified friends or acquaintances as the offender(s) in a substantial portion of the violence that they experienced. Thirty-seven percent of overall violent crime and 46 percent of rapes/sexual assaults were committed by a person the female victim called a friend or acquaintance."
—Bureau of Justice Statistics, *Criminal Victimization 2001*

ANALYSES

The scenario might be that they argue and the bottles are knocked over. She tells him it is over and goes to the closet to get her suitcase to leave. He confronts her and he stabs her in the closet. I don't think it was premeditated. If one is planning to kill an intimate, one does not want to volunteer to be the prime suspect. Killing her in the apartment after the landlady has seen you come in with the victim, and to use your own knife as the weapon, is very poor judgment. Better to kill her outside the apartment with a weapon that cannot be connected to you, or commit the crime in the apartment (as a prostitute she would be known to bring strangers

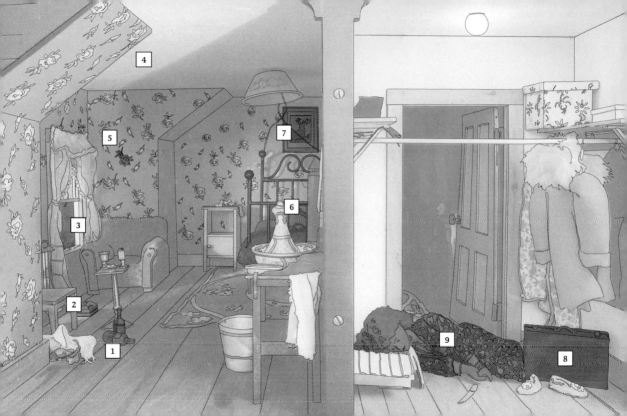

APPENDIX

Interpretations
&
Reviews

The medical examiner designates one of the following five manners of death: natural, suicide, homicide, accident, or undetermined. The following Nutshell cases represent an accidental death, a suicide, two homicides, and an unknown death (because no autopsy was performed). Due to the fact that the models continue to be used to train police officers today, solutions for the other Nutshell cases cannot be revealed.

Saloon and Jail

PATROLMAN MULCAHEY'S STATEMENT WAS CORRECT.

Since Frank Harris died in jail and without attendance by a physician, he became automatically a medical investigator's case. The wound on his forehead was too slight to cause death. A splinter with blood on it was noted on the front corner of the bunk shelf—probably the injury was caused by striking his forehead against this corner when falling. Upon autopsy, the medical investigator found the cause of death to have been a blow to the head received some days before. Police investigation disclosed that Harris had been hit on the head by a timber that was being moved on the dock, where he worked, on Monday afternoon, November 6.

The facts were these: The blow to his head stunned Harris for a time but he soon resumed work. The location of the injury was on the back of his head, low and toward the right side. It raised a lump but, due to his heavy hair and thick cloth cap, did not break the skin. He soon began to have headaches, dizziness and nausea, which became slowly worse, with a feeling of pressure in his head. He continued at work, however, and on Saturday, November 11, was working on the 3 to 11 P.M. shift. Walking home, he felt so dizzy that he thought a drink might help, so went into Pat's Place and had one drink of whiskey. When he came out to the street, he reeled and fell and it was shortly thereafter that the patrolman found him. His death was the result of a slow-seeping hemorrhage into the skull.

Pink Bathroom

Mrs. Fishman had tied the blue cord of her bathrobe tightly around her neck in a square knot. She had climbed up on the stool, put the tasseled ends of the cord over the top of the door, closed the door, and stepped off the stool. This is indicated by the few fine strands of blue cotton thread still adhering to the top edge of the door, which upon microscopic examination were found to be identical to strands of the bathroom cord.

At first sight, this death appeared to be caused by strangulation—inflicted perhaps by someone, possibly the janitor himself, who had climbed in the window from the fire escape—as there appeared to be nothing in the room from which a body could be hung. However, a fact tending to make death by hanging appear possible was the slightly updrawn position of the knot just in front of the left ear. If the investigator had not been very thorough in his scrutiny, the strands of blue cotton on top of the door might easily have been overlooked, and they were the final proof of death by hanging.

NOTE:
When the janitor opened the door, it released the cords, and the fallen body prevented him from opening the door any wider. The reddish discharge from the mouth and nose are characteristic of a body in certain stages of decomposition.

Unpapered Bedroom

This case presents two problems—Who was this woman? And what caused her death?

A small, square pillbox on the dresser, containing ten pink capsules, was promptly noted. The name and address of the pharmacy, the prescription number, and the doctor's name led the investigators to a drugstore on the opposite side of the city. The prescription called for Seconal, and the police chemist determined that the medicine in the pillbox was in fact Seconal, but the box was nearly full and the additional capsules it might have held would not necessarily have constituted a lethal does of that drug.

The doctor signing the prescription identified his patient as Mrs. Mabel Lewis, divorced wife of Walter Lewis and sister of Mrs. Ruth Bailey. When the investigating officers told Mrs. Bailey that "something had happened" to her sister Mabel, Ruth said at once, "Well, what's he done to her this time?" It appears that, in spite of the divorce, the Lewises occasionally spent weekends together, but the affair invariably wound up in a quarrel and Mabel would get a more or less severe beating.

No evidence of violence was found on Mabel's body, but the presence of the drug, together with the empty rum bottle, gave rise to the conjecture that death might have been due to that combination. However, a characteristic condition of the whites of her eyes made the medical examiner suspicious, and a clue was forthcoming when the pillows were examined.

Walter Lewis was soon apprehended and, when confronted with the facts, confessed that he had put the pillow over Mabel's face and held it there until she was quiet and, he presumed, dead, but when he removed it, she was still breathing, so he replaced it for long enough to be sure.

NOTE:
The lipstick prints on the under side of the pillow were the medical examiner's clue.

Two-Story Porch

BOTH STATEMENTS WERE TRUE.

The medical investigator was young—inexperienced—in a hurry. He made a careless and slipshod examination of the body at the scene, *without undressing it*, and gave as a cause of death "fall from a height," failing to recognize that the *cause of the fall* should have been determined.

Annie Morrison's body was taken to Potter and Fields' Undertaking Establishment and, when undressed, there was found to be a bullet hole in the lower part of the right side of the chest twelve inches below the armpit. The police and the chief medical investigator were then brought into the case and an autopsy was performed. This disclosed that, although the bullet had not struck a rib, it had ranged upward at an angle of 45 degrees. The bullet was recovered but was too badly damaged for identification purposes. It was of .22 caliber and Harry Morrison was known to possess a .22 revolver.

A careful reconstruction made it appear that Annie was standing on the green chair facing its back and looking to the right of the observer. This would make it impossible for the shot to have been fired from inside the house. The sharp upward range of the path of the bullet was the determining factor to prove that the shot came from outside the building and from below. Further police investigation brought to light the fact that two boys in the neighborhood had been amusing themselves shooting off a recently acquired .22 rifle and one shot had found its unintended mark in Annie Morrison's body.

Woodman's Shack

The actual cause of death was never established in this case. No autopsy was performed. Discrepancies in reports and statements can be found which were never explained. It is readily evident that this woman could have died from any number of causes, not all of them without possibilities of guilt.

The Nutshell Laboratories have evaluated this case as follows:

FROM THE MEDICAL STANDPOINT:
Dr. Barbour, when making a preliminary investigation to determine whether Ruby was dead, failed to note and report the original position of bedclothes, which might have had bearing on the possibilities of death by suffocation.

This woman might have met her death from (a) natural causes—she had complained of a pain in her neck which could have indicated approaching apoplexy, (b) a blow inflicted by another with similar results, (c) suffocation by means of a pillow or other material at the hands of another, (d) suffocation due to becoming entangled in the bedding because of her drunken condition, (e) poison taken by herself, or, (f) administered by another, (g) exposure and pneumonia, or (h) the consuming of a fatal quantity of alcohol. As it is apparent that no effort was made to eliminate any of these possibilities or to accurately fix upon the correct one, it would appear that Dr. Dombay was in error, to say the least, in not *performing an autopsy*.

FROM THE LEGAL STANDPOINT:
The county attorney has not been provided with any proof of the cause of Wilby Jenks's death. Although Cregg and Stebbiens were present at the time she died, they were in such condition as to make their testimony untrustworthy. In view of all the possibilities listed above, together with the fact that Dr. Barbour could not remember the position of the bedclothes when he first examined the deceased, some positive proof of the cause of death would be requisite before the finding as rendered (death by suffocation) could be considered credible. The county attorney was remiss in not *ordering an autopsy*.

FROM THE POLICE STANDPOINT:

Chief Farmer's report is inadequate in many ways: (a) No description is given of the clothing on the body of Wilby Jenks. If she was dressed as lightly as Dr. Dombay described, in a shack so cold that the men needed mackinaws to keep warm, where was her other clothing and of what did it consist? (b) No information is presented about the clothing worn by the deceased at the time she as "sitting on a chair by the stove" while Cregg "went out to do his chores." If this clothing differed from that found on her dead body, when, by whom, and for what reason was the change made? If the clothing was the same, why was she sitting about in a freezing hut so lightly clad? (c) No mention is made of the presence of a handbag or purse presumably belonging to the dead woman, found lying on the bed. (d) No description is given of the state or possible components of remnants of food found on the table and stove. (e) No account of weather conditions appears in the report. Chief Farmer should not have "pulled the blanket down" until *after* the photographer had made the photograph. He should not have touched or altered anything until *after* photographs, measurements, and descriptions had been recorded. The chief of police was remiss in not *requesting an autopsy.*

FROM THE PHOTOGRAPHIC STANDPOINT:

The four pictures taken demonstrated nothing of value in a court of law. The picture (a) of the outside of the shack has no significance pertinent to the case. Moreover, if the photographer didn't reach the scene until 6:30 P.M. on February 6, and the sun set at 5:03 P.M. EST on that day, it was not possible to take this picture on that day as stated. The picture (b) of the woman's body on the bed was not a representation of conditions as they were first found, but rather of conditions after at least two known alterations had been made. It therefore represented nothing of value and proved nothing. The picture (c) of the man lying on the bed is a posed picture, intended no doubt to show the position in which the man had been lying before the woman's body was removed. Since it was arranged by a photographer who had not witnessed the scene and was posed by a man who, according to all testimony, had been "too drunk to know much about what was going on," its usefulness is nil. The picture (d) of the woman's nude body on the undertaker's table proves nothing beyond the fact that it was nude at the time of taking the photograph. Since there were no marks or wounds to be demonstrated, there appears no valid reason for taking the picture. However, it does disclose some material never included in the reports.

In conclusion, the Nutshell Laboratories wish to respectfully point out that the investigating officials were very generous with their opinions but deficient in their facts. The facts were doubtless readily obtainable by means of autopsy and the three responsible officers were derelict in their duty in not requiring that investigation. This case demonstrated what may happen in rural districts where the services of trained scientific investigators are not always utilized.

ACKNOWLEDGMENTS

I was fortunate to have many people who supported and kept
faith in my project. Most important, I'm grateful to Daniel D'Oca
for helping me in innumerable ways on a daily basis. Without
his unwavering support, advice, intelligence, and love, this book
would not have been possible.

I'm indebted to Susan Enochs for her enthusiasm and for helping
me get this book published. I'm thankful to Elizabeth Kugler, Evan
Schoninger, and everyone at the Monacelli Press for immediately
understanding my vision, and to Michael Worthington and Jon
Sueda for designing a beautiful book.

The Maryland Medical Examiner's Office kindly allowed me to
photograph the Nutshell collection as much as I wanted. Special
thanks to Jerry Dziecichowicz, Chief Administrator; David R.
Fowler, MB, ChB Chief Medical Examiner, State of Maryland;
and Dr. John Smialek (1947–2001), past Chief Medical Examiner.
I also wish to thank the Maryland Medical Legal Foundation; the
Glessner House Museum, particularly Corina Carusi; the staff
of the Rocks estate; and Jack Eckert of the Francis A. Countway
Library of Medicine.

I'm grateful to Jane Shipley for strengthening the essay with her
editorial skills.

Arthur Fournier, Eva Jimenez, and Stacy Morrison also read through
the writing and made excellent suggestions. Daren Kendall and
Jerry Lim generously contributed their talents and time. The following individuals assisted me with information in the line-drawing
section: Dana Kollmann (forensic consultant), Georgeen Theodore,
Tobias Armborst, and Andrea Huelse. I am grateful to Arthur
Bergman, and Richard Ferrari, for their sound advice.

Thanks to those who shared their memories of Frances Glessner
Lee: Percy Lee, Hamilton Lee, John Lee, Percy Langstaff, Frances
Heminway, Virginia Lee, Charles Batchelder, William F. Baker, and
Alton Mosher. I also thank Lee's family for allowing me to quote
from family letters.

Thanks also to Leslie Falk of Collins McCormick, Anna Shteyn-
shleyger, Beth Griffin, Abbott Miller, Rick Woodward, Mr. and
Mrs. D'Oca, Brian Kain, Lori Rubeling, Rosie Shipley, Naomi
Fisher, Frank Benson, Julie Pate, Juan Castro, Jessica Dickinson,
Suzi Gardner, Jonathan Butt, Eileen Kitzis, Jennifer Doublet,
Richard Griffin, and my family.

Above all, I salute Frances Glessner Lee for creating the amazing
crime-scene models.

PHOTO CREDITS

The photographs in this volume are by Corinne May Botz, with
the exception of those on the pages noted below:

14–15: Photograph by Allen Gould, courtesy of the *Boston Herald*
32: Courtesy of the Glessner House Museum, Chicago
34: Reprinted with permission of the *Saturday Evening Post*, c.1949
(Renewed), BFL&MS, Inc., Indianapolis
218–19: Photograph by Allen Gould, courtesy of the *Boston Herald*